이화 한국어

참고서

STUDY GUIDE

이화여자대학교 언어교육원
Ewha Womans University
Ewha Language Center

이화 한국어 참고서

김현진 · 윤여옥 · 이은진 지음

English Version

2-2

EPRESS

이화 한국어 참고서 2-2 (English Version)

지은이 김현진 · 윤여옥 · 이은진

펴낸날 초판 1쇄 2015년 12월 2일
2쇄 2019년 10월 31일
펴낸이 김헌민 **펴낸곳** 이화여자대학교출판문화원
주소 서울특별시 서대문구 이화여대길 52(우 03760) **등록** 1954년 7월 6일 제9-61호
전화 02) 3277-2965(편집), 02) 362-6076(마케팅)
팩스 02) 312-4312 **전자우편** press@ewha.ac.kr **홈페이지** www.ewhapress.com

번역 박경희 · 조윤정 · 한미선 **감수** 최혜원 **진행** 김현진 · 정누리
책임편집 민지영 **디자인** 김리영 · 정혜진 **인쇄** (주)현문자현

ISBN 979-11-5890-127-1 18710
978-89-7300-875-9 (세트)
값 10,000원

* 잘못된 책은 구입처에서 바꾸어 드립니다.

* 이 도서의 국립중앙도서관 출판시도서목록(CIP)은 서지정보유통지원시스템 홈페이지(http://seoji.nl.go.kr)와 국가자료공동목록시스템 (http://www.nl.go.kr/kolisnet)에서 이용하실 수 있습니다.(CIP제어번호: CIP2015031429)

» Contents

Table of Contents

G Grammar P Pronunciation V&E Vocabulary & Expression FE Functional Expression D Dialogue S Script T Text Tell Tell me!

Contents

How to Use This Book

『이화 한국어 참고서 2-1』 and 『이화 한국어 참고서 2-2』 are study guides for Korean-language learners, accompanying the textbooks 『이화 한국어 2-1』 and 『이화 한국어 2-2』. These study guides contain detailed explanations of the grammar, vocabulary and expressions used in the Preparation (준비합시다), Listening (들어 봅시다), Speaking (말해 봅시다), and Reading & Writing (읽고 써 봅시다) sections of each unit. Additionally, the scripts for 들어 봅시다, the dialogues for 말해 봅시다, and the texts for 읽고 써 봅시다 have all been translated into English.

준비합시다

Grammar Focus

Grammar points are clearly explained with morphological information in the table below, helping students to understand the usage of grammatical structures and various irregular forms. Adjectives are marked as A, verbs V, and nouns N. In addition, various examples are given to demonstrate grammar in use.

Focus Plus

More detailed explanations of grammar are given such as the constraints of certain forms or differences with other similar grammatical structures, to help students to reduce errors in using grammatical structures.

Answers

Answers to the exercises in the textbook are given. Students can check the correct answers for themselves.

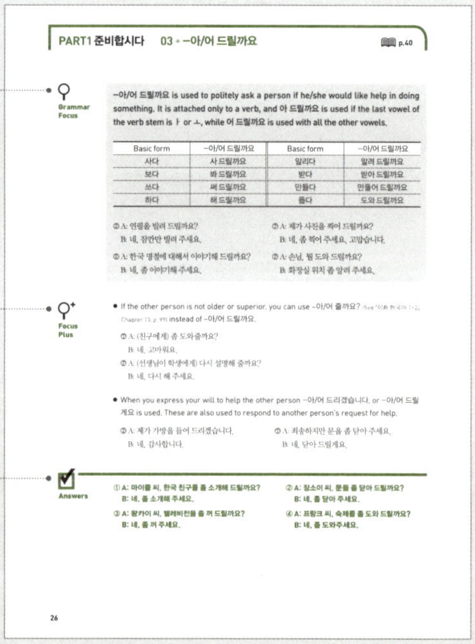

PART1 준비합시다 03 • -아/어 드릴까요 p.40

Grammar Focus

-아/어 드릴까요 is used to politely ask a person if he/she would like help in doing something. It is attached only to a verb, and 아 드릴까요 is used if the last vowel of the verb stem is ㅏ or ㅗ, while 어 드릴까요 is used with all the other vowels.

Basic form	-아/어 드릴까요	Basic form	-아/어 드릴까요
사다	사 드릴까요	알리다	알려 드릴까요
보다	봐 드릴까요	받다	받아 드릴까요
쓰다	써 드릴까요	만들다	만들어 드릴까요
하다	해 드릴까요	돕다	도와 드릴까요

A: 연필을 빌려 드릴까요?
B: 네, 잠깐만 빌려 주세요.

A: 제가 사진을 찍어 드릴까요?
B: 네, 좀 찍어 주세요. 고맙습니다.

A: 한국 명절에 대해서 이야기해 드릴까요?
B: 네, 좀 이야기해 주세요.

A: 손님, 뭘 도와 드릴까요?
B: 화장실 위치 좀 알려 주세요.

Focus Plus

- If the other person is not older or superior, you can use -아/어 줄까요? instead of -아/어 드릴까요.

A: (친구에게) 좀 도와줄까요?
B: 네, 고마워요.

A: (선생님이 학생에게) 다시 설명해 줄까요?
B: 네, 다시 해 주세요.

- When you express your will to help the other person -아/어 드리겠습니다, or -아/어 드릴게요 is used. These are also used to respond to another person's request for help.

A: 제가 가방을 들어 드리겠습니다.
B: 네, 감사합니다.

A: 죄송하지만 문을 좀 닫아 주세요.
B: 네, 닫아 드릴게요.

Answers

① A: 마이클 씨, 한국 친구를 좀 소개해 드릴까요?
B: 네, 좀 소개해 주세요.

② A: 장소이 씨, 문을 좀 닫아 드릴까요?
B: 네, 좀 닫아 주세요.

③ A: 왕카이 씨, 텔레비전을 좀 켜 드릴까요?
B: 네, 좀 켜 주세요.

④ A: 프랑크 씨, 숙제를 좀 도와 드릴까요?
B: 네, 좀 도와주세요.

26

들어 봅시다 / 말해 봅시다 / 읽고 써 봅시다

Vocabulary & Expression

Detailed explanations of meaning and usage are given for words and expressions that are useful in daily life. Various examples are given to increase students' understanding.

Functional Expression

Explanations for functional expressions related with the topic of each section are given in such a way that students can learn to apply them in different situations.

Script / Dialogue / Text

The text for the Listening(들어 봅시다), Speaking(말해 봅시다), Reading & Writing(읽고 써 봅시다) sections in the textbook have been translated into English to help students easily understand the contents.

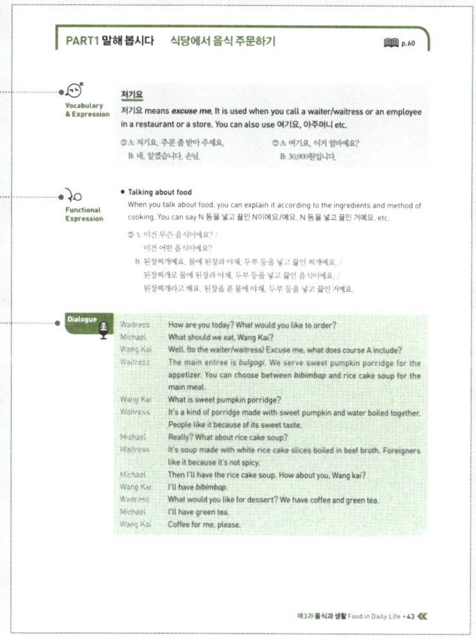

PART1 말해 봅시다 식당에서 음식 주문하기 p.60

Vocabulary & Expression

저기요

저기요 means *excuse me*. It is used when you call a waiter/waitress or an employee in a restaurant or a store. You can also use 여기요, 아주머니 etc.

예 A: 저기요, 주문 좀 받아 주세요.
B: 네, 알겠습니다. 손님.

예 A: 여기요, 이거 얼마예요?
B: 30,000원입니다.

Functional Expression

• Talking about food

When you talk about food, you can explain it according to the ingredients and method of cooking. You can say N 등을 넣고 끓인 N이에요/예요, N 등을 넣고 끓인 거예요, etc.

예 A: 이건 무슨 음식이에요? / 이건 어떤 음식이에요?
B: 된장찌개예요. 물에 된장과 야채, 두부 등을 넣고 끓인 찌개예요. / 된장찌개로 물에 된장과 야채, 두부 등을 넣고 끓인 음식이에요. / 된장찌개라고 해요. 된장을 푼 물에 야채, 두부 등을 넣고 끓인 거예요.

Dialogue

Waitress: How are you today? What would you like to order?
Michael: What should we eat, Wang Kai?
Wang Kai: Well. (to the waiter/waitress) Excuse me, what does course A include?
Waitress: The main entree is *bulgogi*. We serve sweet pumpkin porridge for the appetizer. You can choose between *bibimbap* and rice cake soup for the main meal.
Wang Kai: What is sweet pumpkin porridge?
Waitress: It's a kind of porridge made with sweet pumpkin and water boiled together. People like it because of its sweet taste.
Michael: Really? What about rice cake soup?
Waitress: It's soup made with white rice cake slices boiled in beef broth. Foreigners like it because it's not spicy.
Michael: Then I'll have the rice cake soup. How about you, Wang kai?
Wang Kai: I'll have *bibimbap*.
Waitress: What would you like for dessert? We have coffee and green tea.
Michael: I'll have green tea.
Wang Kai: Coffee for me, please.

제3과 음식과 생활 Food in Daily Life • 43

Answers

Answers to the questions in the Listening(들어 봅시다) and Reading & Writing(읽고 써 봅시다) sections are given along with explanations that will help students to confirm their knowledge and understand the contents.

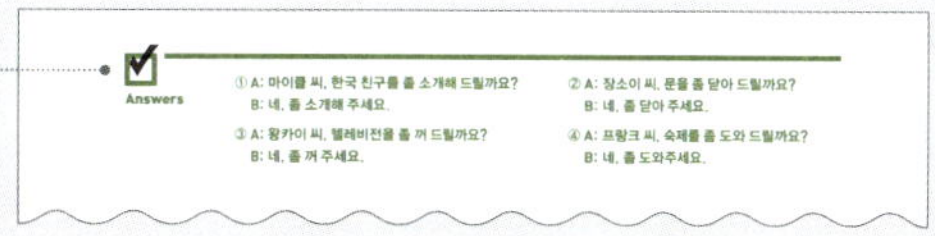

Answers

① A: 마이클 씨, 한국 친구를 좀 소개해 드릴까요?
B: 네, 좀 소개해 주세요.

② A: 장소이 씨, 문을 좀 닫아 드릴까요?
B: 네, 좀 닫아 주세요.

③ A: 왕카이 씨, 텔레비전을 좀 꺼 드릴까요?
B: 네, 좀 꺼 주세요.

④ A: 프랑크 씨, 숙제를 좀 도와 드릴까요?
B: 네, 좀 도와주세요.

Reading & Writing Tip

Explanations are given for the expressions and points to look out for in relation to the contents of the reading and writing exercises in the Reading & Writing(읽고 써 봅시다) section.

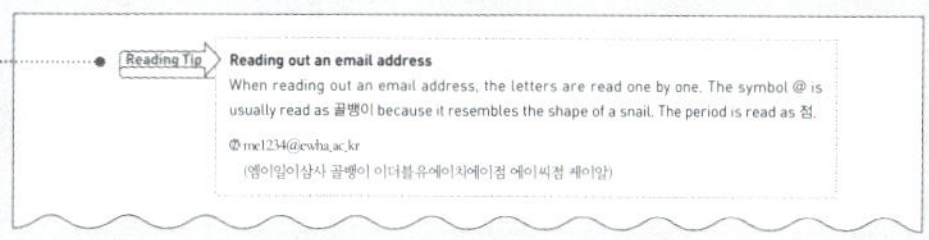

Reading Tip

Reading out an email address

When reading out an email address, the letters are read one by one. The symbol @ is usually read as 골뱅이 because it resembles the shape of a snail. The period is read as 점.

예 me1234@ewha.ac.kr
(엠이일이삼사 골뱅이 이더블유에이치에이점 에이씨점 케이알)

Pronunciation

Explanations are given for the pronunciation rules presented for the reading aloud exercises in the Reading & Writing(읽고 써 봅시다) section along with pronunciation examples.

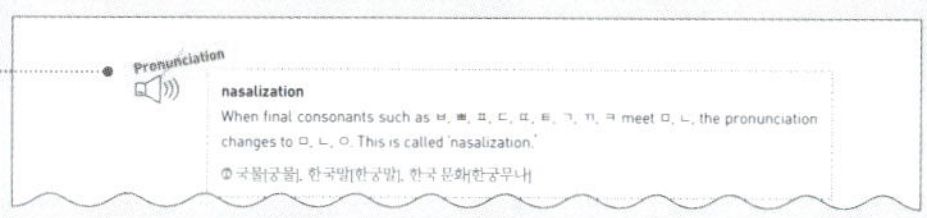

Pronunciation

nasalization

When final consonants such as ㅂ, ㅃ, ㅍ, ㄷ, ㄸ, ㅌ, ㄱ, ㄲ, ㅋ meet ㅁ, ㄴ, the pronunciation changes to ㅁ, ㄴ, ㅇ. This is called 'nasalization.'

예 국물[궁물], 한국말[한궁말], 한국 문화[한궁무나]

Tell me!

Information that is crucial for the study of Korean is given in Q&A form.

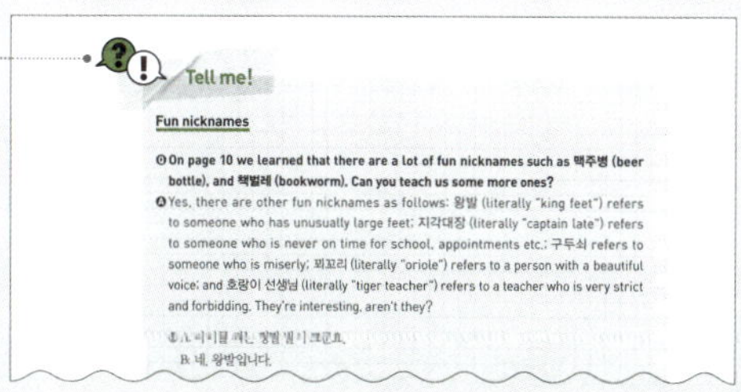

Tell me!

Fun nicknames

Q On page 10 we learned that there are a lot of fun nicknames such as 맥주병 (beer bottle), and 책벌레 (bookworm). Can you teach us some more ones?

A Yes, there are other fun nicknames as follows: 왕발 (literally "king feet") refers to someone who has unusually large feet; 지각대장 (literally "captain late") refers to someone who is never on time for school, appointments etc.; 구두쇠 refers to someone who is miserly; 꾀꼬리 (literally "oriole") refers to a person with a beautiful voice; and 호랑이 선생님 (literally "tiger teacher") refers to a teacher who is very strict and forbidding. They're interesting, aren't they?

예 A: [illegible]
B: 네, 왕발입니다.

Vocabulary Check

A basic vocabulary list is given for each unit taking into account the frequency and level of difficulty of words. The words are grouped into various categories according to the overall topic of each unit, helping the students to memorize the vocabulary and test themselves.

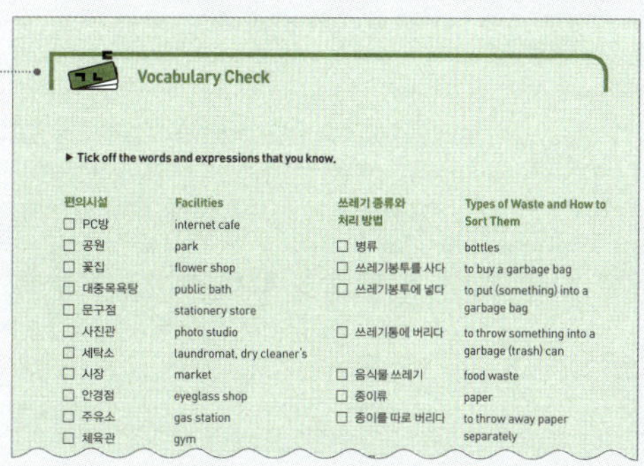

Vocabulary Check

▶ Tick off the words and expressions that you know.

편의시설	Facilities	쓰레기 종류와 처리 방법	Types of Waste and How to Sort Them
□ PC방	internet cafe	□ 병류	bottles
□ 공원	park	□ 쓰레기봉투를 사다	to buy a garbage bag
□ 꽃집	flower shop	□ 쓰레기봉투에 넣다	to put (something) into a garbage bag
□ 대중목욕탕	public bath		
□ 문구점	stationery store		
□ 사진관	photo studio	□ 쓰레기통에 버리다	to throw something into a garbage (trash) can
□ 세탁소	laundromat, dry cleaner's		
□ 시장	market	□ 음식물 쓰레기	food waste
□ 안경점	eyeglass shop	□ 종이류	paper
□ 주유소	gas station	□ 종이를 따로 버리다	to throw away paper separately
□ 체육관	gym		

Grammar Focus

–고 있다 is used when the result of a completed action is ongoing. It is usually attached to verbs such as 입다, 신다, 쓰다, 매다, 끼다, 들다, etc. It is used whether the verb stem ends in a consonant or a vowel.

Basic form	–고 있다	Basic form	–고 있다
쓰다	쓰고 있다	입다	입고 있다
매다	매고 있다	신다	신고 있다
끼다	끼고 있다	들다	들고 있다

ex A: 장소이 씨는 무슨 옷을 입고 있어요?
B: 장소이 씨는 스웨터하고 청바지를 입고 있어요.

ex A: 마이클 씨는 어떤 옷을 입었어요?
B: 반바지를 입고 모자를 쓰고 있어요.

ex A: 여기 있는 사람 중에서 이치로 씨가 누구예요?
B: 이치로 씨는 저기 창가에 있는 사람이에요. 양복을 입고 넥타이를 매고 있는 사람요.

ex A: 저기 배낭을 메고 손에 책을 들고 있는 사람이 누구예요?
B: 수잔 씨예요. 제 친구예요.

ex A: 얀 씨, 이 사진에서 배낭을 메고 부츠를 신고 있는 사람이 누구예요?
B: 우리 누나예요. 5년 전쯤인 것 같아요.

Focus Plus

- –고 있다 is also used when a certain action is in progress. When a certain action was in progress in the past, –고 있었다, which is the past tense form of –고 있다, is used. In this case, it is only combined with verbs. (See 「이화 한국어 1–2」 Chapter 9, p.38)

ex A: 수잔 씨, 지금 뭐 하고 있어요?
B: 지금 책 읽고 있어요.

ex A: 어제 제가 전화했을 때 뭐 하고 있었어요?
B: 그때 텔레비전을 보고 있었어요.

Answers

① A: 리처드 씨는 무슨 옷을 입고 있어요?
B: 리처드 씨는 양복을 입고 넥타이를 매고 있어요.

② A: 나타샤 씨는 무슨 옷을 입고 있어요?
B: 나타샤 씨는 원피스를 입고 장갑을 끼고 있어요.

③ A: 프랑크 씨는 무슨 옷을 입고 있어요?
B: 프랑크 씨는 티셔츠와 반바지를 입고 운동화를 신고 있어요.

④ A: 진차오 씨는 무슨 옷을 입고 있어요?
B: 진차오 씨는 재킷을 입고 가방을 들고 있어요.

⑤ A: 율리아 씨는 무슨 옷을 입고 있어요?
B: 율리아 씨는 치마를 입고 가방을 메고 있어요.

Grammar Focus

-게 is used to express the method or degree of a following action or situation. It is attached to an adjective and is used whether the adjective stem ends in a consonant or a vowel.

Basic form	-게	Basic form	-게
싸다	싸게	쉽다	쉽게
예쁘다	예쁘게	작다	작게
시원하다	시원하게	짧다	짧게
멋있다	멋있게	맵지 않다	맵지 않게

ex A: 아저씨, 이 바지 얼마예요?
B: 5만 원이에요.
A: 네? 좀 싸게 주세요.

ex A: 오늘 날씨 어때요? 추워요?
B: 네, 추워요. 옷을 따뜻하게 입고 나가세요.

ex A: 이 사과 어떻게 할까요? 씻을까요?
B: 네. 깨끗하게 씻어 주세요.

ex A: 바지를 어떻게 고쳐 드릴까요?
B: 좀 기니까 3cm 정도 짧게 해 주세요.

ex A: 마이클 씨, 회사에 새로 온 사람은 어떻게 생겼어요?
B: 키도 크고 멋있게 생겼어요.

ex A: 선생님, 그 문법을 잘 모르겠어요. 쉽게 한 번 더 설명해 주시겠어요?
B: 네, 알겠어요. 잘 들어 보세요.

Answers

① A: 여자 친구가 어떻게 생겼어요?
B: 귀엽고 예쁘게 생겼어요.

② A: 잘 들려요?
B: 아니요, 잘 안 들려요. 좀 더 크게 말씀해 주세요.

③ A: 뭘 이렇게 많이 차리셨어요?
B: 차린 것은 없지만 맛있게 드세요.

④ A: 설명을 들었으니까 이제 이해할 수 있겠지요?
B: 아니요. 죄송하지만 다시 쉽게 설명해 주시겠어요?

Grammar Focus

처럼 is used when a certain shape or action is similar to or the same as that of the preceding noun. 처럼 is only attached to a noun, which is the subject of comparison.

Noun	처럼	Noun	처럼
어머니	어머니처럼	인형	인형처럼
가수	가수처럼	생각	생각처럼
영화배우	영화배우처럼	한국 사람	한국 사람처럼

ex A: 티엔 씨, 지금 사는 하숙집은 어때요?
B: 아주 좋아요. 아주머니가 어머니처럼 따뜻하게 돌봐 주세요.

ex A: 요코 씨는 노래를 잘해요?
B: 네. 정말 가수처럼 잘해요.

ex A: 율리아 씨는 한국말을 언제까지 공부할 거예요?
B: 한국 사람처럼 말할 때까지 공부하고 싶어요.

ex A: 얀 씨, 한국 생활은 어때요?
B: 처음에는 걱정을 많이 했어요. 그런데 생각처럼 힘들지 않은 것 같아요.

ex A: 영민 씨 조카는 어떻게 생겼어요?
B: 인형처럼 귀엽고 예쁘게 생겼어요.

ex A: 수잔 씨 동생은 키가 커요?
B: 제 남동생요? 농구 선수처럼 커요.

Focus Plus

- 처럼 can be replaced with 같이 without a significant difference in meaning.

ex 아이가 말을 꼭 어른처럼 해요.
(= 어른같이)

이 침대는 모양이 자동차처럼 생겼어요.
(= 자동차같이)

Answers

① A: 미셸 씨는 한국말을 잘해요?
B: 네, 한국 사람처럼 잘해요.

② A: 박현미 씨는 날씬해요?
B: 네, 미스코리아처럼 날씬해요.

③ A: 티엔 씨는 예쁘게 생겼어요?
B: 네, 인형처럼 예쁘게 생겼어요.

④ A: 이치로 씨는 발음이 정확해요?
B: 네, 아나운서처럼 정확해요.

⑤ A: 나타샤 씨는 노래를 잘 불러요?
B: 네, 가수처럼 노래를 잘 불러요.

Vocabulary & Expression

인상착의

인상착의 means ***a person's features and dress***. In other words, it means how a person looks and what he/she wears. It is used in expressions such as 인상착의를 설명하다 and N와/과 인상착의가 비슷하다.

ex A: 내일 공항에서 만날 남자의 인상착의를 설명해 주세요.
B: 키가 작고 약간 통통해요. 그리고 티셔츠에 청바지를 입고 있을 거예요.

ex A: 장소이 씨, 혹시 어제 이화백화점에 갔어요?
B: 아니요. 그런데 왜요?
A: 어제 제가 백화점에서 장소이 씨와 인상착의가 비슷한 사람을 본 것 같아서요.

ex A: 김민호 씨, 어제 저를 찾아온 분의 인상착의가 어땠어요?
B: 키는 보통이고 머리는 갈색이었어요. 그리고 파란색 스웨터를 입고 있었어요.

넥타이를 맨 사람

넥타이를 맨 사람 means ***a person wearing a tie***. 매다 means to fasten a string or cord by making a diagonal loop and pulling the ends to make a knot, or to wrap something around the body and make a knot so that it does not come loose. It is used in expressions such as 신발 끈을 매다, 넥타이를 매다, 가방에 리본을 매다. Therefore, 넥타이를 맨 사람 means a person wearing a tie. On the other hand, 메다 means to put something over one's shoulder.

ex A: 저기 하늘색 넥타이를 맨 사람이 누구예요?
B: 마이클 씨예요. 성격도 좋고 노래도 잘해서 인기가 많아요.

ex A: 이 와이셔츠에 무슨 색 넥타이를 맬까요?
B: 파란색 넥타이를 매 보세요. 어울릴 것 같아요.

ex A: 그 배낭은 손에 들지 말고 어깨에 메세요.
B: 네, 그렇게 할게요.

Functional Expression

- **Expressing disagreement with another person's opinion**

When you don't agree with what another person says, you can indirectly express your disagreement by saying 글쎄요, 잘 모르겠어요 or directly express your disagreement by saying 네?, 진짜 그렇게 생각해요?, 정말 그렇게 생각하세요? A difference in opinion can also be expressed by repeating what the other said.

ex A: 마이클 씨가 정말 멋있지요?
B: 글쎄요. 잘 모르겠어요. / 네? 마이클 씨가 멋있어요? /
진짜 그렇게 생각해요? 전 아닌 것 같아요. / 정말 그렇게 생각하세요? 글쎄 잘 모르겠어요.

Script

Zhang Souyi	Jeongmin, congratulations on your graduation!
Jeongmin	Thank you. Oh, the guy I told you about the other time, Cheolsu, whom I want to introduce to you, is here at the graduation ceremony. That's him standing by the tree.
Zhang Souyi	The guy wearing a suit and tie?
Jeongmin	No, he's my senior. Do you see the man beside him? The guy wearing cotton pants, a shirt, and glasses is Cheolsu. Isn't he handsome?
Zhang Souyi	What? Do you think he's handsome? I don't think so.
Jeongmin	Really? Then who do you like most among the people here?
Zhang Souyi	Well, I think the guy behind the chair looks quite nice.
Jeongmin	Who? The man holding a bouquet of flowers?
Zhang Souyi	Yes. He's tall like a model and well-dressed. He also seems fun to talk to.
Jeongmin	Ah, Minho? He's already got a girlfriend.

Answers

(1) ② Cheolsu is the man who is beside the tree and wearing cotton pants, a shirt, and glasses. The man who is like a model, well-dressed and holding a bouquet of flowers is Minho.

(2) ② Lee Jeongmin's senior is the man who is wearing a suit and tie.

(3) ② Zhang Souyi likes Minho. Minho is behind the chair, holding a bouquet of flowers. Therefore, ② is Minho.

Tell me!

Expressions for color

Q Among the expressions for color, what is the difference between 연분홍색 and 분홍색? What expression is used for a color darker than pink?

A 분홍색 is the term used for the color pink, while 연분홍색 refers to pale or light pink. A darker shade of pink is referred to as 진분홍색. The expressions 연하다 and 진하다 are also used to indicate 'weak' and 'strong,' respectively. For example, when talking about coffee, weak coffee containing a lot of water is described as 연한 커피 while coffee with a strong flavor and aroma is described as 진한 커피.

ex A: 나타샤 씨는 분홍색을 좋아하는 것 같아요.
B: 네. 저는 분홍색 중에서도 진분홍색을 좋아해요. 이 지갑도 진분홍색이 마음에 들어서 샀어요.

ex A: 왕카이 씨, 커피는 어떤 걸로 마실래요?
B: 전 연한 걸로 주세요. 진한 커피를 마시면 밤에 잠이 잘 안 와요.

친구 마중 부탁하기

p.24

Vocabulary & Expression

갑자기

갑자기 means ***suddenly***. It means that something happens quickly and unexpectedly, before one has time to think.

ex A: 지금 밖에 비가 와요?
B: 네. 조금 전까지는 날씨가 맑았어요. 그런데 갑자기 비가 오네요.

다행이네요

다행이네요 means that something is lucky or fortunate. It is used when something goes against expectations and turns out well.

ex A: 어제 학교 앞에서 교통사고가 났어요. 혹시 알고 계세요?
B: 네. 그때 학교 앞에 있어서 봤어요. 그런데 다친 사람이 없었어요. 참 다행이지요.

Functional Expression

- **Asking someone to go and meet a person (in your place)**
  When you ask someone to go meet a visitor in your place, you can say 마중갈 수 있어요?, 마중을 부탁해도 돼요?, 마중 가는 게 가능해요?, or 마중하러 나가 줄 수 있어요?, etc.

ex A: 영민 씨가 마중갈 수 있어요? /
영민 씨에게 마중을 부탁해도 돼요? /
영민 씨, 혹시 마중 가는 게 가능해요? /
영민 씨가 마중하러 나가 줄 수 있어요?
B: 그럼요. 제가 마중하러 갈게요.

Dialogue

Michael	Yeongmin, are you free this afternoon?
Park Yeongmin	Yes. What's up?
Michael	Well, my friend is coming to Korea today and I was supposed to go and meet her. But something urgent has come up and I'm afraid I can't make it. Can you go and meet my friend for me?
Park Yeongmin	Sure, I'll do it. But what does she look like?
Michael	She's as pretty as a movie star. She's small. She'll be wearing jeans and a T-shirt and sneakers. Her name is Alice.
Park Yeongmin	Alice? Does she speak Korean well?
Michael	Yes, she studied Korean for a long time in the US, so she speaks like a Korean.
Park Yeongmin	That's good. Can you write down the flight number here?
Michael	It's KE321, arriving at 4:30.
Park Yeongmin	All right. I'll call you as soon as I meet her.

Grammar Focus

마다 means 'each and every.' In other words, it is used when each and every situation is similar or when each situation repeats itself. 마다 is only attached to a noun and it does not change its form whether the noun ends in a consonant or a vowel.

Noun	마다	Noun	마다
나라	나라마다	식당	식당마다
학교	학교마다	사람	사람마다

ex A: 티엔 씨, 보통 아침에 일어나서 뭐 해요?
B: 저는 아침마다 신문을 읽고 식사해요.

ex A: 수잔 씨는 산을 좋아하세요?
B: 네, 저는 산을 좋아해요. 그래서 매년 가을마다 단풍 구경하러 설악산에 가요.

ex A: 장소이 씨, 이 옷이 우리 일본의 전통의상이에요.
B: 그래요? 나라마다 전통의상이 다 멋있네요.

ex A: 이 식당은 무슨 요일에 쉬어요?
B: 여기는 일요일마다 쉬어요.

ex A: 요코 씨와 저는 이번 일에 대한 생각이 다른 것 같아요.
B: 그럼요. 사람마다 생각이 달라요. 같은 게 더 이상하죠.

ex A: 경주에 가는 버스는 몇 분마다 있어요?
B: 경주행 버스는 30분마다 있어요.

Focus Plus

- There are idiomatic expressions such as 날마다 and 해마다. 날마다 means every day and 해마다 means every year.

  ex A: 날마다 학교에 가야 돼요?
  B: 아니요. 매일 가지 않아요. 일주일에 세 번 가요.

  ex A: 마이클 씨, 고향에는 일 년에 몇 번 가요? 해마다 가요?
  B: 특별히 바쁜 일이 없으면 해마다 가려고 해요.

Answers

① 매일 아침마다 조깅해요.

② 4년마다 올림픽이 열려요.

③ 식당마다 음식 맛이 달라요.

④ 나라마다 인사 방법이 달라요.

Grammar Focus

The 'ㅎ Drop' refers to the dropping of the final ㅎ by some adjectives with stems ending in ㅎ when they are followed by an ending that begins with 으. In addition, if an ending that begins with –아/어 comes after ㅎ, the ㅎ from the stem drops off and the –아/어 of the ending changes to 애 or 얘 with the vowels of the last syllable of the stem. However, 어떻다 changes to 어때요 and 그렇다 changes to 그래요.

Basic form	–아/어요	–아/어서	–(으)ㄴ	–습니다
빨갛다	빨개요	빨개서	빨간	빨갛습니다
파랗다	파래요	파래서	파란	파랗습니다
하얗다	하얘요	하얘서	하얀	하얗습니다
그렇다	그래요	그래서	그런	그렇습니다
동그랗다	동그래요	동그래서	동그란	동그랗습니다

ex A: 무슨 색 꽃을 좋아해요?
B: 저는 빨간색 꽃을 좋아해요. 특히 빨간 장미가 제일 좋아요.

ex A: 우산을 잃어버렸어요. 혹시 교실에서 노란 우산 못 봤어요?
B: 저기 책상 서랍에 있는 거 아니에요?

ex A: 티엔 씨, 밖을 보세요. 하늘이 정말 맑고 파래요.
B: 정말 그러네요. 한국의 가을은 정말 멋있어요.

ex A: 마이클 씨에게는 어떤 안경이 어울릴까요?
B: 글쎄요. 얼굴이 동그래서 네모난 안경도 좋을 것 같아요.

ex A: 어디 아파요? 얼굴이 너무 하얘요.
B: 그래요? 배탈이 나서 그럴 거예요.

Focus Plus

- Adjective stems ending in ㅎ including 좋다, 많다, 싫다, 괜찮다 are regular adjectives. All others ending in ㅎ are classified as irregular adjectives.

  ex A: 오늘 날씨가 어때요?
  B: 좋아요. 하늘도 맑고 파래요.

Answers

① A: 장례식에 갈 때 보통 무슨 옷을 입어요?
B: 보통 까만 정장을 입어요.

② A: 티엔 씨가 어떻게 생겼어요?
B: 동그란 얼굴에 눈이 커서 귀엽게 생겼어요.

③ A: 마이클 씨가 많이 아픈 것 같아요.
B: 맞아요. 얼굴이 너무 하얘요.

④ A: 어젯밤에 첫눈이 왔어요.
B: 그래요? 저는 일찍 자서 못 봤어요.

⑤ A: 무슨 계절을 가장 좋아하세요?
B: 하늘이 높고 파래서/파란 가을이 제일 좋아요.

Vocabulary & Expression

데리고 있는 분

데리고 있는 분 means ***a person who has something/someone close by***. 데리고 있다 means to have one's inferior or an animal close by. Therefore, 데리고 있는 분 means a person who keeps an inferior or animal close by his/her side. On the other hand, 모시고 있다 means to be close by the side of someone superior while 가지고 있다 is used for an object, not a person or animal.

ex (게시판에서)

- 강아지를 찾고 있어요. 하얀색 강아지입니다. 혹시 데리고 있는 분은 연락 주세요. (☎ 010-3753-1000)

ex A: 민호 씨, 서울에서 혼자 살아요?
B: 아니요. 대학교에 다니는 동생을 데리고 있어요.

ex A: 수진 씨는 우리 모임에 잘 못 나오는 것 같아요. 무슨 일 있어요?
B: 수진 씨가 아픈 어머니를 모시고 있어요. 그래서 외출을 잘 안 해요.

지퍼

지퍼 means ***zipper***. It is made by sewing strips of metal or plastic teeth side by side on fabric tape so that the teeth interlock and the two rows of teeth are separated or fastened as you pull or push a small sliding piece along them. It is usually used to open and close pants, skirts, jackets, pockets, wallets or bags.

ex A: 바람이 불어서 날씨가 쌀쌀해요. 점퍼에 있는 지퍼를 올리세요.
B: 네, 그래야겠어요.

ex A: 수잔 씨, 좀 도와줄래요? 배낭 지퍼가 안 열려요.
B: 그러네요. 지퍼가 고장 난 것 같아요.

장식

장식 means ***decoration*** or ***ornamentation*** and refers to the embellishment of dishes, furniture, clothing, and other items with pieces of metal, fabric, plastic, and other materials in a variety of shapes and patterns.

ex A: 우리 언니가 결혼식에서 입은 드레스 어땠어요?
B: 반짝이는 장식이 많이 있어서 아주 화려했어요.

ex A: 이 도자기가 참 예쁘지요?
B: 네. 특히 뚜껑에 꽃 장식이 예뻐서 인기가 많겠어요.

Functional Expression

- **Requesting someone to come upon hearing an announcement**

  You can say 듣는 즉시 와 주세요, 들으면 바로 와 주세요, 들으시면 빨리 와 주세요 when you ask someone to come as soon as he/she hears an announcement.

  ex (안내 방송에서)

  이 방송을 듣는 즉시 1층으로 와 주세요. /
  이 방송을 들으면 바로 1층으로 와 주세요. /
  이 방송을 들으시면 1층으로 빨리 와 주세요.

Script

We are looking for a dog. It is a brown chihuahua. It has big, black eyes, a short tail and long legs. It is wearing a red bell around its neck and a pink ribbon on its head. Anyone who has seen or is keeping the dog, please contact the information desk at the main entrance.

We are looking for the parents of a five-year-old boy. His name is Park Minsu. He has a pale face and short hair. He is wearing a white T-shirt, blue pants and sky-blue sneakers. He is also wearing a yellow backpack. When his parents hear this announcement, please come to the broadcasting room as soon as possible.

We are looking for a bag lost near the restrooms. It is black with a zipper decorating every pocket. Inside the bag are a red diary, a white handkerchief, and a book. There is a student ID in the diary. If anyone has seen or is keeping this bag, please call the broadcasting room or information desk.

Answers

(1) ②

The first announcement is about a lost dog. The dog is a brown chihuahua wearing a pink ribbon on its head and a red bell around its neck.

(2) ③

The second announcement is looking for the parents of a lost five-year-old boy. The boy is wearing a white T-shirt, blue pants, and sky-blue sneakers. He is also wearing a yellow backpack.

(3) ① 네 ② 아니요 ③ 아니요

The third announcement is looking for a lost bag. It is black and has zipper decorations on the pockets. There is a handkerchief, diary, and a book in the bag. The student ID is not in the red wallet, but in the red diary.

분실물 센터에서 잃어버린 물건 찾기

p.30

Vocabulary & Expression

잃어버렸어요

잃어버렸어요 means ***(I) lost it***. It indicates that one has lost something unwittingly or has become separated from someone who was with him/her or going somewhere together. On the other hand, 잊어버리다 means that one has forgotten something one used to know.

ex A: 어제 복잡한 백화점에서 지갑을 잃어버렸어요.
B: 그래요? 지갑에 돈이 많이 들어 있었어요?

ex A: 저기에서 다른 사람에게 종이를 나눠 주는 사람이 우리 앞집 아주머니 아니에요?
B: 맞아요. 저 아주머니가 지난달에 강아지를 잃어버렸어요. 그래서 찾는 광고 종이를 나눠 주고 있는 거예요.

Functional Expression

- **Saying that one's missing item is not in the lost-and-found**

When you have lost something, you may go to the lost-and-found to ask if your missing item is there. You may be told that your missing item is not there. In this case, you may be told 아직 그런 N은/는 안 들어왔습니다, 여기에 지금 그런 N은/는 없습니다, 찾고 있는 N이/가 없어요 or 저희가 가지고 있는 N 중에는 없습니다.

ex (분실물 센터에서)
A: 오늘 아침에 파란색 가죽 지갑을 잃어버렸어요. 혹시 그런 지갑이 있나요?
B: 아직 그런 지갑은 안 들어왔습니다. /
여기에 지금 그런 지갑은 없습니다. /
찾고 있는 지갑이 없어요. /
저희가 가지고 있는 지갑 중에는 없습니다.

Dialogue

Staff	Can I help you?
Zhang Souyi	Yes, please. I lost my wallet at school this morning. I looked for it in every classroom but I couldn't find it. Is there a black wallet here?
Staff	What does it look like?
Zhang Souyi	It is long and rectangular.
Staff	Wait a minute, please. Is this it?
Zhang Souyi	No, it's leather, not fabric. Also, there's a circular decoration on it.
Staff	I'm afraid we don't have your wallet here.
Zhang Souyi	There's a student ID and ARC card in it, so I have to find it as soon as possible.
Staff	I see. I will call you when your wallet comes in. Please write down your name and phone number here.
Zhang Souyi	All right. Please call me if you find it.

Vocabulary & Expression

이상형

이상형 means ***an ideal type***. It is the most perfect type of person one can think of.

ex A: 왕카이 씨는 이상형이 어떻게 돼요?
B: 저는 키가 크고 성격이 활발한 여자를 좋아해요.

ex A: 저 사람이 장소이 씨 이상형에 가까워요?
B: 네, 외모는 그런 것 같아요. 그런데 성격은 아직 잘 모르겠어요.

ex A: 나타샤 씨, 나타샤 씨는 남편이 이상형이었어요?
B: 그렇지는 않았어요. 제 이상형은 영화배우처럼 잘생긴 사람이었어요. 제 남편은 잘생기지는 않았지만 성격도 좋고 저를 잘 이해해 줘서 결혼했어요.

눈이 높은 걸까?

눈이 높은 걸까? means ***(am I) aiming too high?*** 눈이 높다 means that one tends to seek something better than others or one has very sophisticated tastes. It is usually used when choosing a person or item.

ex A: 저 선배는 왜 여자 후배들에게 인기가 있을까요? 전 별로인데요.
B: 멋있지 않아요? 티엔 씨, 너무 눈이 높은 거 아니에요?

ex A: 수잔 씨, 수잔 씨는 눈이 너무 높아요.
B: 제가요? 그렇지 않아요. 저는 잘생기고 운동 잘하고 성격 좋은 사람을 찾는 거예요.
A: 그게 바로 눈이 높은 거예요. 그런 사람은 없어요.

ex A: 이것보다 저쪽에 있는 게 더 좋은 것 같아요. 저걸로 보여 주세요.
B: 손님, 눈이 높으시네요. 이것보다는 저게 훨씬 비싸고 디자인도 세련된 것입니다.

말이 잘 통했다

말이 잘 통했다 means ***(we) spoke/talked the same language***. This expression means that two people are communicating well or that a conversation went smoothly as the people concerned had similar thoughts or opinions.

ex A: 고등학교 때 얀 씨하고 친했죠? 늘 같이 다닌 거 같아요.
B: 네. 우리는 정말 말이 잘 통했어요.

ex A: 우리 반 친구들 중에서 누구하고 제일 말이 잘 통해요?
B: 왕카이 씨요. 취미도 비슷하고 나이도 같아서 같이 있으면 아주 편하고 좋아요.

ex A: 제 발음이 이상한 것 같아요. 한국 사람들과 말이 잘 안 통해요.
B: 그래요? 이상하지 않아요. 괜찮아요.

Pronunciation

Elimination of the final consonant ㅎ

When a vowel follows the final consonants ㅎ, ㄶ, and ㅀ, [ㅎ] is not pronounced.

ex 않았고 [아날꼬], 않았다[아날따], 좋았다[조앋따], 좋은[조은]

Text

Someone Different from My Ideal Type

A My ideal type is a tall and handsome man like a movie star. I like a man who is well-dressed like a model. Since I am very into fashion, I also want my boyfriend to be interested in fashion. I would like him to be active and kind but I don't want him to be kind to other women. I like a man who is nice only to me. Plus, I want him to have a job that is flexible so that we can see each other more frequently. Am I aiming too high? Maybe this is why I don't have a boyfriend yet.

B This was because he looked different from my ideal type. He was neither tall nor handsome. Besides, he was wearing a yellow shirt that didn't suit him. So my first impression of him was not good.

C Then yesterday, my friend introduced me to a man. Before I met him, my friend said, "He's a really great guy." So I had high expectations but when I met him, I was disappointed.

D But contrary to what I had first thought, we were able to talk easily. We had a pleasant talk and I found out that he has an active personality. Also he was a very nice man. I realized that you should not judge a person by appearance before getting to know him or her.

Answers

(1) (C), (B), (D)

A is followed by a story about one's own experience. The beginning of the new story is C. At this time, the sentence usually starts with 그런데 to indicate a change of subject. Following C, there is an explanation of why the writer was disappointed. Therefore, B follows. Then, the writer's thoughts come at then end, which is D.

(2) ① 아니요 ② 네 ③ 네

The writer does not particularly care about a man's job. She did not like the looks of the man she was introduced to but did like his personality and as they talked she found out his good points.

(3) 외모: 키가 크지 않고 얼굴도 잘생기지 않았습니다.
옷차림: 어울리지 않는 노란색 셔츠를 입고 있습니다.
성격: 성격이 활발하고 좋습니다. 아주 친절합니다.

Vocabulary Check

▶ **Tick off the words and expressions that you know.**

색	Colors
☐ 하얀색(= 흰색)	white
☐ 노란색	yellow
☐ 연두색	light green
☐ 초록색(= 녹색)	green
☐ 주황색	orange
☐ 빨간색	red
☐ 하늘색	sky-blue
☐ 파란색	blue
☐ 연분홍색	pale pink
☐ 분홍색	pink
☐ 자주색	purple
☐ 보라색	violet
☐ 갈색	brown
☐ 밤색	chestnut brown
☐ 회색	gray
☐ 까만색(= 검정색)	black
☐ 금색	gold
☐ 은색	silver

옷차림	Attire
☐ 가방을 들다	to hold a bag
☐ 귀걸이를 하다	to wear a pair of earrings
☐ 꽃다발을 들다	to hold a bouquet of flowers
☐ 넥타이를 매다	to put on a tie
☐ 머리띠를 하다	to wear a hairband
☐ 목걸이를 하다	to wear a necklace
☐ 목도리를 하다	to wear a muffler
☐ 반바지를 입다	to wear shorts
☐ 반지를 끼다	to wear a ring
☐ 배낭을 메다	to put on/wear a backpack
☐ 브로치를 하다	to wear a brooch
☐ 스카프를 하다	to wear a scarf
☐ 시계를 차다	to wear a watch
☐ 안경을 쓰다	to wear glasses
☐ 양말을 벗다	to take off socks
☐ 양말을 신다	to put on socks
☐ 장갑을 끼다	to put on gloves
☐ 장갑을 벗다	to take off gloves
☐ 코트를 입다	to put on a coat
☐ 팔찌를 하다	to wear a bracelet

옷	Clothing
☐ 긴팔 옷	long-sleeved clothes
☐ 긴팔	long sleeves
☐ 등산복	hiking clothes
☐ 등산화	hiking boots
☐ 면바지	cotton pants
☐ 미니스커트	miniskirt
☐ 민소매 티셔츠	sleeveless shirt
☐ 반바지	shorts
☐ 반팔 티셔츠	short-sleeved T-shirt
☐ 부츠	boots
☐ 샌들	sandals
☐ 선글라스	sunglasses
☐ 셔츠	shirt
☐ 수영복	swimsuit
☐ 스웨터	sweater
☐ 양복	suit
☐ 원피스	dress
☐ 장화	rain boots
☐ 점퍼	jacket
☐ 정장	formal attire
☐ 청바지	jeans
☐ 카디건	cardigan
☐ 코트	coat

PART1 준비합시다 01 • (이)나, 밖에

p.38

Grammar Focus

(이)나 is used to show that an amount is more than expected or quite sufficient. 밖에 is used to show that an amount is less than expected. 밖에 is usually followed by a negative expression. (이)나 and 밖에 are both attached to a noun, and 이나 is used if the noun ends in a consonant, while 나 is used if it ends in a vowel. 밖에 does not change its form whether the noun ends in a consonant or a vowel.

Noun	(이)나	Noun	밖에
반	반이나	하나	하나밖에
열 권	열 개나	두 개	두 권밖에

ex A: 점심 먹었어요?
B: 네. 방금 먹고 왔어요. 너무 배가 고파서 밥을 두 그릇이나 먹었어요.

ex A: 왜 그렇게 옷을 많이 샀어요?
B: 지금 백화점에서 세일을 해서 치마를 다섯 개나 샀어요.

ex A: 어제 잘 잤어요?
B: 아니요. 어제 시험공부 때문에 2시간밖에 못 잤어요.

ex A: 미셸 씨는 안경이 몇 개 있어요?
B: 다섯 개밖에 없어요.
A: 와, 다섯 개나 있어요?

Answers

① A: 마이클 씨는 매일 몇 시간 자요?
B: 저는 일곱 시간이나 자요.
A: 그래요? 일곱 시간밖에 안 자요?

② A: 마이클 씨는 한 달에 책을 몇 권 읽어요?
B: 저는 두 권밖에 안 읽어요.
A: 그래요? 두 권이나 읽어요?

③ A: 마이클 씨는 하루에 몇 시간 운동해요?
B: 저는 한 시간밖에 운동 안 해요.
A: 그래요? 한 시간이나 해요?

④ A: 마이클 씨는 하루에 커피를 몇 잔 마셔요?
B: 저는 세 잔이나 마셔요.
A: 그래요? 세 잔밖에 안 마셔요?

⑤ A: 마이클 씨는 한 달에 용돈으로 얼마 받아요?
B: 저는 오십 만원밖에 안 받아요.
A: 그래요? 오십 만원이나 받아요?

Grammar Focus

-(으)면서 is used to indicate that one person is doing more than one behavior at the same time. It is usually attached to a verb and -으면서 is used if the verb stem ends in a consonant, while -면서 is used if it ends in a vowel or the consonant ㄹ. The subject in the first clause with -(으)면서 must be the same as that of the following clause. In such cases, the subject is generally omitted in the second clause.

Basic form	-(으)면서	Basic form	-(으)면서
가다	가면서	듣다	들으면서
오다	오면서	만들다	만들면서
입다	입으면서	돕다	도우면서
읽다	읽으면서	짓다	지으면서

ex A: 아침에 보통 뭐 해요?
B: 저는 아침에 뉴스를 보면서 아침밥을 먹어요.

ex (미용실에서)
A: 지금 머리를 할 수 있어요?
B: 아니요. 이 잡지를 읽으면서 잠시만 기다려 주시겠어요?

ex A: 동생은 지금 어디에 있어요?
B: 욕실에 있어요. 음악을 들으면서 샤워하고 있을 거예요.

ex 나는 회사에 다니면서 한국어를 공부했어요. (○)
나는 회사에 다니면서 그는 한국어를 공부했어요. (×)
나는 회사에 다니면서 나는 한국어를 공부했어요. (×)

Focus Plus

- (이)면서 is used with a noun and indicates that the subject is in a certain state while maintaining another state at the same time. It is usually used to show that the subject maintains two conditions at the same time such as identity, social position, or profession.

  ex A: 마이클 씨는 무슨 일을 해요?
  B: 마이클 씨는 학생이면서 회사원이에요.

Answers

① A: 미셸 씨는 지금 뭐 하고 있어요?
B: 커피를 마시면서 신문을 보고 있어요.

② A: 나타샤 씨는 지금 뭐 하고 있어요?
B: 요리를 하면서 전화를 받고 있어요.

③ A: 장소이 씨는 지금 뭐 하고 있어요?
B: 노래를 부르면서 춤을 추고 있어요.

④ A: 왕카이 씨는 지금 뭐 하고 있어요?
B: 샌드위치를 먹으면서 컴퓨터를 하고 있어요.

 p.40

Grammar Focus

-(으)ㄴ/는데 is used in roughly three situations. First, it is used to present a background or previous situation in order to introduce a certain fact or relate specific details. Second, it is used to present a reason or grounds for the following clause. Third, it is used when the opposite result or situation to the previous clause comes in the following clause or to talk about two contrasting facts. It is attached to an adjective or a verb. -은데 is used if the adjective stem ends in a consonant, while -ㄴ데 is used if it ends in a vowel or the consonant ㄹ. In the case of verbs, -는데 is used whether the verb stem ends in a consonant or a vowel. -았/었는데 is used for a past fact. In the past tense form, -았는데 is used if the last vowel of the stem of the adjective or verb is ㅏ or ㅗ, and -었는데 is used with all the other vowels.

Basic form	-(은)ㄴ데	-았/었는데	Basic form	-는데	-았/었는데
크다	큰데	컸는데	가다	가는데	갔는데
작다	작은데	작았는데	입다	입는데	입었는데
좋다	좋은데	좋았는데	살다	사는데	살았는데
덥다	더운데	더웠는데	묻다	묻는데	물었는데
멀다	먼데	멀었는데	돕다	돕는데	도왔는데
그렇다	그런데	그랬는데	짓다	짓는데	지었는데

ex A: 저 지금 편의점에 가는데 뭐 필요한 거 있어요?
B: 그래요? 그럼 물을 마시고 싶은데 물 좀 사다 주세요.

ex A: 비가 올 것 같은데 우산 하나 삽시다.
B: 네. 그게 좋겠어요.

ex A: 어제 영화 봤어요?
B: 아니요, 영화관에 갔는데 표가 매진돼서 못 봤어요.

ex A: 가족들이 매운 음식을 잘 먹어요?
B: 저는 매운 음식을 잘 먹는데 우리 부모님은 잘 못 드세요.

Answers

① A: 미셸 씨는 운동을 좋아해요?
B: 네. 운동을 좋아하는데 요즘은 바빠서 운동을 자주 못 하는 것 같아요.

② A: 미셸 씨는 한국 요리를 잘해요?
B: 네. 한국 요리를 잘하는데 특히 된장찌개를 맛있게 끓여요.

③ A: 미셸 씨는 하숙집에서 살아요?
B: 네. 하숙집에서 사는데 미셸 씨 집은 학교에서 좀 멀어요.

④ A: 미셸 씨는 모자가 많아요?
B: 네. 모자가 많은데 모자 중에서 빨간색 야구 모자를 제일 좋아하는 것 같아요.

⑤ A: 미셸 씨는 티엔 씨와 이번 학기에 같은 반이에요?
B: 네. 티엔 씨와 이번 학기에 같은 반인데 지난 학기에도 두 사람은 같은 반이었어요.

Vocabulary & Expression

돌잔치와 돌잡이

돌잔치 is a party held to celebrate a baby's first birthday. The parents invite friends and relatives to attend and the invited guests usually bring baby clothes, money, or gold rings as birthday gifts. During 돌잡이, the parents put several things on a table to predict the baby's future from the item that the baby grabs. The usual *doljabi* items are 돈, 마패, 벼루, 붓, 연필, 실, 쌀, 판사 봉, 화살, 활. However, these days things such as 마이크, 청진기, 컴퓨터 마우스 are also included. Changes in the times have brought changes to the items used, and traditional *doljabi* items such as 마패, 붓, 벼루, 화살, and 활 are no longer popular. People make a prediction about the baby's future profession according to the item that he/she grabs.

ex A: 내일 친구 아이의 돌잔치가 있어서 가려고 하는데 무슨 선물을 준비하면 좋을까요?
B: 보통 아이 옷이나 금반지를 많이 선물해요.

ex A: 돌잡이 물건에는 무슨 뜻이 있어요?
B: 실을 잡으면 건강하게 오래 살고 붓이나 연필을 잡으면 공부를 잘할 거라고 생각해요.

놓아요

놓아요 means ***to put something down, lay something down***. 놓다 is to put an object down on the surface of something. Another verb that looks similar to 놓다 is 넣다, which is to put an object inside a drawer, bag, wallet etc.

ex A: 돌잡이 물건으로 상 위에 보통 무엇을 놓아요?
B: 보통 실이나 돈, 쌀, 연필을 놓아요.

ex A: 가방을 책상 아래에 놓으세요.
B: 네, 알겠습니다.

ex A: 책과 필통을 가방 안에 모두 넣으세요.
B: 네, 알겠습니다.

ex A: 지갑 안에 신용카드를 넣었지요?
B: 네, 아까 식당에서 계산한 후에 지갑에 넣었어요.

Functional Expression

- **Saying that one would like to go somewhere if there is an opportunity**
When you want to say that you would like to go somewhere if there is an opportunity, after hearing another person's story or suggestion, you can say 기회가 되면 저도 가 보고 싶어요, 여유가 되면 한 번 가 보고 싶네요, 시간이 있으면 한번 가고 싶네요 etc.

ex A: 이번 휴가 때 제주도에 다녀왔는데 너무 좋았어요.
B: 그래요? 저도 기회가 되면 가 보고 싶어요. /

정말요? 저도 여유가 될 때 갔으면 좋겠어요. /
그래요? 저도 기회가 있으면 한번 가고 싶네요. /
그렇군요. 저도 여유가 되면 한번 가 보고 싶어요. /
그렇군요. 저도 시간이 있으면 한번 가 보고 싶네요.

Script

Zhang Souyi	Junyeong, did you have a good weekend?
Han Junyeong	Yes, I went to my nephew's *doljanchi*.
Zhang Souyi	*Doljanchi*? What's that?
Han Junyeong	We call a baby's first birthday *dol*. To celebrate, we invite friends and relatives to a party called *doljanchi* and eat lots of good food. We also perform *doljabi* in front of the guests. Do you know what that is?
Zhang Souyi	No, I don't. What is *doljabi*?
Han Junyeong	We put silk or cotton thread, rice, and pencils on a table and let the baby grab what he/she wants to predict the baby's future.
Zhang Souyi	Interesting. What do the *doljabi* items mean?
Han Junyeong	If the baby grabs thread it means a long and healthy life, rice means wealth, the pencil means great intelligence, and so on. But these days people even add items such as a computer mouse or stethoscope. We placed five items on the table including a stethoscope but my nephew grabbed money.
Zhang Souyi	It must have been fun. I've never been to a *doljanchi*. I'd love to go to one someday.
Han Junyeong	Yes, you really should go once.

Answers

(1) ③

Han Junyeong attended his nephew's *doljanchi*, which is a party held to celebrate a baby's first birthday. Han Junyeong did not go to a friend's birthday party or a party to predict a baby's future.

(2) ①

Han Junyeong's nephew grabbed money. It is said that grabbing money means wealth in the future.

(3) ① 아니요 ② 네 ③ 아니요

Han Junyeong went to his nephew's first birthday party called *doljanchi*. For the *doljabi* ceremony there were as many as five objects such as thread, money, rice, a pencil, and a stethoscope. Zhang Souyi has never been to a *doljanchi*.

야유회 옷차림에 대한 조언 구하기

p.43

Vocabulary & Expression

그러세요

그러세요 means ***please do so***. It is an expression to show that you agree with what the other person is about to do and to tell the person to do as he/she pleases. You can also say 그렇게 하세요.

ex A: 유키 씨, 안녕하세요? 유키 씨 옆에 앉아도 될까요?
B: 네, 그러세요.
(= 그렇게 하세요)

ex A: 제가 우리 반 친구들에게 반 모임 장소를 알려 줄게요.
B: 네, 그러세요. 그럼 저는 선생님께 알려 드릴게요.

Functional Expression

- **Giving advice regarding someone's attire**

When you give advice regarding someone's attire, you can say N을/를 입는 게 좋아요, N을/를 많이 입어요, N이/가 어울리니까 그걸 입는 게 어때요? etc.

ex A: 결혼식에 갈 때 어떻게 입는 게 좋을까요?
B: 보통 정장을 많이 입어요. /
정장 차림을 하는 게 좋아요. /
정장을 입고 가는 게 좋아요. /
치마 정장이 잘 어울리니까 그걸 입는 게 어때요?

Dialogue

Zhang Souyi	Hyeonmi, what are you wearing to the picnic this weekend?
Park Hyeonmi	It's hot, so I'm going to wear shorts. What about you?
Zhang Souyi	I'm going to wear long pants. I have five pairs of pants but I don't have any shorts.
Park Hyeonmi	Long pants should be okay. But do you have a hat? The sun is very strong these days and you'll probably need a hat.
Zhang Souyi	Really? Then I'll buy one when I go shopping in Myeong-dong tomorrow.
Park Hyeonmi	Yes, you should. You should try to pick a hat that goes well with your clothes when you're shopping tomorrow.
Zhang Souyi	Do I need anything else?
Park Hyeonmi	Oh, you should bring a long-sleeved shirt. When the sun goes down, it gets a little chilly.
Zhang Souyi	Really? Then I'll bring a long-sleeved shirt as well.
Park Hyeonmi	That's a good idea.

Grammar Focus

You can put two or more particles together according to a certain order. Some examples are 에도, 에만, 에서도, 에서만, (으)로도, (으)로만, 한테도, and 한테만.

Noun	에서도	에서만	Noun	에도	에만
학교	집에서도	집에서만	학교	학교에도	학교에만
한국	한국에서도	한국에서만	서울	서울에도	서울에만
Noun	(으)로도	(으)로만	Noun	한테도/에게도	한테만/에게만
버스	버스로도	버스로만	친구	친구한테도	친구한테만
지하철	지하철로도	지하철로만	동생	동생에게도	동생에게만

ex A: 이번 한국 여행 어땠어요? 부산에도 가 봤어요?
B: 아니요. 시간이 없어서 서울에만 갔어요.

ex A: 집에서도 공부해요?
B: 아니요. 집에서는 공부가 안 돼서 도서관에서만 공부해요.

ex A: 미셸 씨의 결혼 소식을 반 친구들에게도 이야기했어요?
B: 아니요. 마이클 씨한테만 이야기했어요.

ex A: 인천에 버스로만 갈 수 있어요?
B: 아니요. 지하철로도 갈 수 있어요.

ex A: 예약은 전화로만 해야 돼요?
B: 아니요. 인터넷으로도 할 수 있어요.

Focus Plus

- Particles such as 이/가 and 을/를 are not used with other particles.

ex 요코 씨가 공부해요. 미셸 씨도 공부해요.(○)
요코 씨가 공부해요. 미셸 씨가도 공부해요.(×)

ex 요코 씨가 한국어를 공부해요. 그리고 영어도 공부해요.(○)
요코 씨가 한국어를 공부해요. 그리고 영어를도 공부해요. (×)

Answers

① 아니요. 김포공항에서도 출발해요.

② 아니요. 부산에도 가요.

③ 아니요. 3층에는 없어요. 1층에만 있어요.

④ 아니요. 휴대 전화로만 연락했어요.

⑤ 아니요. 인터넷으로도 할 수 있어요.

Grammar Focus

–고 나서 indicates that some other action is taken or a certain situation occurs after finishing a certain action. It is attached to a verb and is used whether the verb stem ends in a consonant or a vowel.

Basic form	–고 나서	Basic form	–고 나서	Basic form	–고 나서
가다	가고 나서	만들다	만들고 나서	돕다	돕고 나서
입다	입고 나서	묻다	묻고 나서	짓다	짓고 나서

ex A: 오늘 수업 끝나고 영화 보러 갈래요?
B: 수업 끝나고 숙제를 해야 해요. 숙제를 하고 나서 가는 게 어때요?

ex A: 라면을 끓일 때 면을 언제 넣어야 돼요?
B: 물이 끓고 나서 넣는 게 좋아요.

ex A: 언제 도서관에 갈 거예요?
B: 점심을 먹고 나서 도서관에 가려고요.

Focus Plus

- –고 나서 can be replaced with –(으)ㄴ 후에 (See 『이화 한국어 1–2』 Chapter 9, p.42) or –(으)ㄴ 다음에. Additionally, it can be replaced with –고서, which also indicates that the previous clause is the cause or reason for the following clause.

ex A: 언제 운동하러 갈까요?
B: 숙제하고 나서 운동하러 갑시다.
(= 숙제한 후에, 숙제한 다음에, 숙제하고서)

ex A: 유키 씨, 몸은 좀 괜찮아요?
B: 네, 고향에서 가져온 약을 먹고서 감기가 다 나았어요.
(= 먹었어요. 그래서)

Answers

① A: 언제 청소할 거예요?
B: 빨래를 하고 나서 청소를 할 거예요.

② A: 언제 모임 장소로 출발할 거예요?
B: 이 일을 끝내고 나서 모임 장소로 출발할 거예요.

③ A: 언제 부모님 선물을 사러 갈 거예요?
B: 은행에서 돈을 찾고 나서 부모님 선물을 사러 갈 거예요.

④ A: 언제 친구에게 답장을 쓸 거예요?
B: 친구에게서 전화를 받고 나서 친구에게 답장을 쓸 거예요.

⑤ A: 언제 고향에 돌아갈 거예요?
B: 6급까지 한국어 수업을 마치고 나서 고향에 돌아갈 거예요.

Vocabulary & Expression

부모님 댁

부모님 댁 means ***parents' house***. 댁 is an honorific way of speaking of someone else's house or family. Some examples are 할머니 댁, 할아버지 댁, 아버지 댁, 선생님 댁, 사장님 댁.

ex A: 이번 추석에 어디에 가요?
B: 시골에 계신 할아버지 댁에 가요.

ex A: 선생님, 이번 주말에 댁으로 찾아 봬도 될까요?
B: 네, 오세요.

부모님에게 절을 하는 거예요

부모님에게 절을 하는 거예요 means ***(we) bow to our parents***. It means to bow down to one's parents as a sign of respect. 절(을) 하다 does not indicate bowing by simply lowering the head but kneeling and bowing low with the head touching the ground.

ex A: 어른이 계신 한국인 친구 집에 가는데 어떻게 인사해야 돼요?
B: 어른이 계시면 어른에게 절을 하는 게 좋아요.

ex A: 신혼여행 다녀와서 뭐 했어요?
B: 신혼여행에서 돌아와서 한복을 입고 부모님 댁에 갔어요. 그리고 부모님에게 절했어요.

정말 그래도 돼요?

정말 그래도 돼요? means ***can (I) really do that?*** It is used to ask if one can really do what the other person says. It is used when you are surprised and ask if it's really okay to do what the other person says.

ex A: 이번 방학에 괜찮으면 부산에 있는 저희 집에 놀러 오세요.
B: 정말 그래도 돼요?

ex A: 이번 주말에 다른 계획이 없으면 저랑 같이 제 조카 돌잔치에 갈래요?
B: 정말 그래도 돼요?

Functional Expression

- **Expressing New Year's greetings**

Around the year-end holidays, people exchange New Year's greetings with relatives or close acquaintances as a way to bring the end of the year to a close. Several different New Year's greetings such as 새해 복 많이 받으세요, 새해 복 많이 받으시고 건강하세요, 한 해 마무리 잘 하시고 행복한 새해 되세요 are used.

ex A: 새해 복 많이 받으세요. / 새해 복 많이 받으시고 건강하세요. /
한 해 마무리 잘 하시고 행복한 새해 되세요. / 새해에는 더 행복하시고 건강하시길 바랍니다.
B: 네, 고맙습니다. 새해 복 많이 받으세요.

Script

Park Yeongmin	Michael, New Year's Day is coming up next week. Do you have any plans?
Michael	No, not yet. What about you?
Park Yeongmin	I am going to my parents' house.
Michael	That's good. By the way, what do Korean people usually do on New Year's Day?
Park Yeongmin	The whole family gets together on New Year's Day. We observe a rite for the ancestors in the morning and eat rice cake soup. And then we bow to our parents, which is called *sebae*.
Michael	*Sebae*? What's that?
Park Yeongmin	It's a New Year's ritual bow. We bow to our grandparents and parents. And when we bow, we always say "May the New Year bring you much good fortune."
Michael	I see.
Park Yeongmin	If you don't have any other plans, Michael, why don't you come over to our house?
Michael	Can I really do that?
Park Yeongmin	Of course. Ever since I mentioned you, my family has wanted to meet you. Let's eat delicious food and play *yutnori*(traditional Korean game) together.
Michael	Thanks for inviting me. I promise to go.

Answers

(1) ③

On Korean New Year's Day, people bow to their parents and other adults, but not to their friends.

(2) ①

Michael is going to Park Yeongmin's house on New Year's Day. The two friends will eat good food at Park Yeongmin's house and play *yutnori* with the family.

(3) ① 네　② 네　③ 아니요

After we observe a rite for the ancestors in the morning, we eat rice cake soup. For a New Year's greeting, we bow to our grandparents and parents and say "May the New Year bring you much good fortune."

Vocabulary & Expression

글쎄요

글쎄요 means ***well, maybe.*** It is a vague answer to another person's question or request.

ex A: 우리 이번 방학에 함께 여행하기로 했지요? 어디에 가고 싶어요?
B: 글쎄요. 아직 특별히 생각한 곳은 없는데 우리 지금 같이 정해 볼까요?

ex A: 내일 우리 모임에 나와 줄 수 있어요?
B: 글쎄요. 내일 다른 모임이 있는데, 그 모임이 일찍 끝나면 갈 수 있고 늦게 끝나면 못 갈 것 같아요.

Functional Expression

- **Asking about holiday plans**

When asking about holiday plans, you can say 연휴에 뭐 할 거예요?, 연휴에 좋은 계획이 있어요?, or 이번 연휴에 무슨 계획이 있어요?

ex A: 연휴에 뭐 할 거예요? /
연휴에 좋은 계획이 있어요? /
이번 연휴에 무슨 계획이 있어요? /
이번 연휴에 특별한 계획이 있어요?
B: 글쎄요. 아직 잘 모르겠어요.

Dialogue

Zhang Souyi	Ichiro, what are you doing during the Chuseok holidays?
Ichiro	Well, I'm not really sure yet. What about you?
Zhang Souyi	I'm going to read, listen to music, and rest at home on the first day of the long holiday.
Ichiro	Really? Then what about the next day?
Zhang Souyi	I'm going to go to the traditional Hanok Village. If you go there, you can make *songpyeon* to eat and play traditional games.
Ichiro	I see. But do they have Chuseok events at Hanok Village only?
Zhang Souyi	No, they also have Chuseok events at Gyeongbokgung and Seoul Plaza.
Ichiro	At Seoul Plaza too?
Zhang Souyi	Yes, they have traditional mask dance performances. After looking around the Chuseok events at Hanok Village, I'm going to head to Seoul Plaza.
Ichiro	It sounds like fun.
Zhang Souyi	Then do you want to come with me?
Ichiro	Yes, I'd like that. I'm already looking forward to it.

Vocabulary & Expression

제기차기

제기차기 means a traditional Korean game where people compete in kicking the *jegi* (a shuttlecock with tassels) into the air as many times as possible without letting it touch the ground. 제기 is a traditional Korean children's toy. It is used in expressions such as 제기차기를 하다 or 제기를 차다.

ex 제기차기는 제기를 차면서 노는 한국의 전통놀이인데 명절이 되면 한옥 마을 행사에서 제기차기 하는 것을 볼 수 있다.

ex 우리는 제기차기를 해서 제기를 가장 많이 찬 사람에게 선물을 주기로 했다.

두세 번

두세 번 means ***two, three times***. Saying two numbers in a row to indicate an approximate number is as follows.

1~2	한두	4~5	네다섯
2~3	두세	5~6	대여섯
3~4	서너	6~7	예닐곱

ex 어제 줄넘기를 했는데 두세 번밖에 못했다.

ex 해야 할 공부가 많았는데 시간이 없어서 서너 시간밖에 못했다.

정말 의미 있는 시간이었다

정말 의미 있는 시간이었다 means ***it was such a meaningful time***. It indicates a precious and special time. It is an expression used when a certain experience or matter is very valuable and significant. 의미 있는 시간 can be replaced with 뜻깊은 시간.

ex 이번 여행은 나에게 정말 의미 있는 시간(= 뜻깊은 시간)이었다.

ex 선생님과 함께 보낸 날들은 우리에게 정말 의미 있는 시간(= 뜻깊은 시간)이었다.

Reading & Writing Tip

How to write a diary

Since writing a diary is talking about yourself, you do not have to intentionally write 나는 very often. However, when you do have to use 나는, be careful not to write 저는 or 제가.

ex (일기 쓸 때) 나는 박물관을 구경했고 동생은 호텔에서 쉬었다. (○)
(일기 쓸 때) 저는 박물관을 구경했고 동생은 호텔에서 쉬었다. (×)
(일기 쓸 때) 제가 박물관을 구경했고 동생은 호텔에서 쉬었다. (×)

Text

Friday, October 6

Today is Chuseok. Since I wanted to experience Chuseok firsthand, my classmate Ichiro and I went to Hanok Village.

At Hanok Village, there were lots of people wearing *hanbok*, which really made it feel like a holiday. We first went to the place where they were making *songpyeon*. The *songpyeon* that I had this morning at the boarding house were white, but there they had *songpyeon* in many colors such as yellow, green, wine etc. The different colored *songpyeon* had different tastes. But I liked the green ones the best. After we had *songpyeon*, we went to the place where we were able to try on *hanbok*. This event was very popular, so we had to wait more than 30 minutes. After 30 minutes, we put on the *hanbok* and took pictures.

Next, we went to see the traditional games. I particularly wanted to try *jegichagi* since I had learnt about it in class. But it was trickier than I thought and almost everybody was able to kick the shuttlecock only a few times. However, Ichiro kicked it as many as ten times and got a big round of applause from the audience.

As I ate *songpyeon* and played traditional games today, I felt close to Korean people and what Korean culture was all about. It was such a meaningful time. Even after I go back to China, I think I will never forget the experience that I had today.

Pronunciation

Pronunciation of 의

When 의 is the first letter of a word it is pronounced as [의], and in all other cases it is pronounced as either [의] or [이]. As a particle, when 의 comes behind a noun, it is written as 의 but pronounced as either [의] or [에].

ex 의미[의미], 거의[거의],[거이], 사람들의[사람들의],[사람드레], 오늘의[오늘의],[오느레]

Answers

(1) ②

Zhang Souyi once learnt about *jegichagi* in class.

(2) ① 네 ② 네 ③ 아니요

Since the *hanbok* event was very popular, they had to wait for over 30 minutes before they could try the *hanbok* on. Also, Ichiro kicked the *jegi* as many as ten times and got a round of applause.

(3) (2), (4), (3)

When Zhang Souyi and Ichiro went to Hanok Village, they first went to the place where they could make *songpyeon*. After eating *songpyeon*, they went to the place where they were able to try on *hanbok*. They took pictures wearing the *hanbok*. Then they went to the traditional games section and played *jegichagi*.

Vocabulary Check

▶ **Tick off the words and expressions that you know.**

설날	New Year's Day (Seollal)
☐ 떡국을 먹다	to eat *tteokguk* (rice cake soup)
☐ 새해 인사를 하다	to make New Year's greetings
☐ 세배를 하다	to bow to elders on New Year's Day
☐ 세뱃돈을 받다	to receive money as a New Year's gift

추석	Chuseok
☐ 보름달을 구경하다	to see the full moon
☐ 소원을 빌다	to make a wish
☐ 송편을 만들다	to make *songpeyon* (crescent-shaped rice cakes)
☐ 햇과일을 먹다	to eat newly harvested fruit

명절	Holidays
☐ 가족들이 모이다	to have the family gather together
☐ 선물을 교환하다	to exchange gifts
☐ 성묘를 하다	to visit to one's ancestral graves
☐ 전통 놀이를 하다	to play traditional games
☐ 차례를 지내다	to hold memorial services for one's ancestors
☐ 칠면조 고기를 먹다	to eat turkey
☐ 크리스마스트리를 만들다	to decorate a Christmas tree
☐ 폭죽을 터뜨리다	to pull the firecrackers
☐ 한복을 입다	to wear *hanbok* (traditional Korean costume)

전통놀이	Traditional Games
☐ 널뛰기	seesawing
☐ 씨름	*ssireum* (wrestling)
☐ 연날리기	kite-flying
☐ 윷놀이	*yutnori* (traditional board game)
☐ 제기차기	game of shuttlecock
☐ 투호	*tuho* (throwing arrows into a jar)

생일잔치	Birthday Party
☐ 돌잔치	first birthday party
☐ 손님을 초대하다	to invite guests
☐ 음식을 차리다	to set the table
☐ 촛불을 끄다	to put out candles
☐ 촛불을 켜다	to light candles
☐ 칠순잔치	70th birthday party
☐ 케이크를 자르다	to cut the cake
☐ 환갑(회갑)	60th birthday party

돌잡이 물건	*Doljabi* Items
☐ 공(농구공, 축구공, 골프공 등)	ball (basketball, soccer ball, golf ball etc.)
☐ 돈	money
☐ 마이크	microphone
☐ 벼루	inkstone
☐ 붓	writing brush
☐ 실	string
☐ 쌀	rice
☐ 연필	pencil
☐ 청진기	stethoscope
☐ 컴퓨터 마우스	computer mouse
☐ 판사봉	judge's gavel
☐ 화살	arrow
☐ 활	bow

특별한 날	Special Days
☐ 결혼기념일	wedding anniversary
☐ 결혼식	wedding
☐ 소풍	picnic
☐ 송년회	year-end party
☐ 송별회	farewell party
☐ 야유회	picnic
☐ 집들이	housewarming party
☐ 체육대회	athletics carnival
☐ 추수감사절	Thanksgiving Day
☐ 크리스마스	Christmas
☐ 할로윈데이	Halloween

PART1 준비합시다 01 • -는 대로

p.56

Grammar Focus

-는 대로 is used when an action or state in the previous clause is directly followed by another action or state in the following clause. It is attached to a verb and is used only when the situations or actions in the previous and following clauses are closely related. Past tense verbs cannot be used in the following clause, which is generally about a schedule, plan, request, or demand. In the previous clause, negative expressions such as 안, 못, -지 않다, -지 못하다 cannot be used.

Basic form	-는 대로	Basic form	-는 대로
가다	가는 대로	열다	여는 대로
쓰다	쓰는 대로	듣다	듣는 대로
먹다	먹는 대로	돕다	돕는 대로
읽다	읽는 대로	짓다	짓는 대로

ex A: 언제 미셸 씨 생일 선물을 사러 갈까요?
B: 오늘 수업이 끝나는 대로 같이 가요.

ex A: 마이클 씨를 만나는 대로 이 메모를 좀 전해 주세요.
B: 네, 알겠습니다.

ex A: 그 책을 다 읽으면 좀 빌려 주세요.
B: 네, 좋아요. 다 읽는 대로 빌려 줄게요.

ex A: 배가 고파요. 언제 밥을 먹어요?
B: 조금만 기다리세요. 잡채를 다 만드는 대로 함께 먹어요.

ex 집에서 나오는 대로 학교에 갈 것이다. (○)
집에서 나오는 대로 비가 내렸다. (×)

Answers

① A: 이치로 씨, 언제 보고서를 작성할 거예요?
B: 자료를 찾는 대로 작성할 거예요.

② A: 장소이 씨, 언제 은행에 들를 거예요?
B: 수업이 끝나는 대로 들를 거예요.

③ A: 프랑크 씨, 언제 약속 장소를 알려 줄 거예요?
B: 장소를 예약하는 대로 알려 줄 거예요.

④ A: 왕카이 씨, 언제 친구에게 사진을 보내 줄 거예요?
B: 사진을 정리하는 대로 보내줄 거예요.

⑤ A: 나타샤 씨, 언제 도서관에 책을 빌리러 갈 거예요?
B: 학생증을 만드는 대로 빌리러 갈 거예요.

02 • –(으)ㄹ 것

p.57

Grammar Focus

–(으)ㄹ 것 is used when you tell yourself or someone else what to do. It is used to briefly convey instructions or directions in note form and hence is usually applied to memos, statements, or public notices. It is attached to a verb and if the verb stem ends in a consonant –을 것 is used, while –ㄹ 것 is used if it ends in a vowel or the consonant ㄹ. The negative form is –지 말 것.

Basic form	–(으)ㄹ 것	–지 말 것
오다	올 것	오지 말 것
만나다	만날 것	만나지 말 것
먹다	먹을 것	먹지 말 것
만들다	만들 것	만들지 말 것
돕다	도울 것	돕지 말 것
듣다	들을 것	듣지 말 것
짓다	지을 것	짓지 말 것

ex (선생님이 학생에게)
"수업 시간에는 한국어로만 이야기하세요."

> 수업 시간에는
> 한국어로만 이야기할 것.

ex (호텔 직원이 손님에게)
"건물 안에서는 담배를 피우지 마세요."

> 건물 안에서는
> 담배를 피우지 말 것.

ex (사장님이 직원에게)
"회의 준비가 되면 연락해."

> 회의 준비가 되면
> 연락할 것.

ex (나 자신에게)
"수업에 가기 전에 이 자료를 모두 읽자."

> 수업에 가기 전에
> 이 자료를 모두 읽을 것.

Answers

① 외출할 때 컴퓨터를 끌 것.
② 수업 후에 이메일을 꼭 확인할 것.
③ 냉장고 문을 잘 닫을 것.
④ 사람이 많은 곳에 가지 말 것.
⑤ 애완동물을 키우지 말 것.

Vocabulary & Expression

비자를 연장해야 하는데

비자를 연장해야 하는데 means ***(I) need to extend my visa.*** 비자를 연장하다 is to extend the period of temporary residence beyond the original date. And 비자를 신청하다 is to formally request the organization concerned to issue a visa. 비자를 심사하다 is to review whether one is eligible for a visa. 비자가 나오다, or 비자가 발급되다 means that the organization concerned has issued a visa.

ex A: 중국에 여행을 가려고 해요. 뭐가 필요해요?
B: 여행 비자가 필요해요. 여행사에 비자를 신청하세요.

ex A: 유학 준비는 다 됐어요?
B: 아직요. 미국 대사관에서 비자를 심사하는 중이에요.

ex A: 벌써 비자가 나왔어요?
B: 네. 신청한 지 5일 만에 비자가 발급됐어요.

학교에 신청하세요

학교에 신청하세요 means ***(you should) apply for it at school.*** It indicates that you should request that the school do something for you. When you formally ask an organization or agency to perform a certain task you can say N에 신청하다.

ex A: 학생증을 잃어 버렸어요. 어떻게 해야 해요?
B: 학교에 신청하세요. 학생증을 다시 받을 수 있어요.

ex A: 제가 사려는 가방이 백화점에 없어요. 어디에서 살 수 있을까요?
B: 인터넷으로 살 수 있어요. 백화점 홈페이지에 주문 신청하세요.

수입 인지

수입 인지 means ***revenue stamps.*** They are stamps issued by the government to collect taxes. They are affixed to an item or document as proof that the government tax or fee has been paid.

ex A: 운전면허 시험을 보려고 해요. 뭐가 필요해요?
B: 신청서에 사진하고 수입 인지를 붙여야 돼요.

Functional Expression

- **Asking if something is possible**

When you ask if it is okay for you to do something, you can say –아/어도 돼요? or –(으)면 안 돼요?, –아/어도 괜찮아요?

ex A: 거기에 아침 일찍 가도 돼요? / 거기에 아침 일찍 가면 안 돼요? / 거기에 아침 일찍 가도 괜찮아요?
B: 너무 일찍 오시면 안 돼요. 오전 10시에 문을 열어요.

- **Responding modestly to a compliment or gratitude**

  In response to another person's compliment or gratitude, you can say 뭘요, 아니에요, 별말씀을요 to modestly express that what you did was no big deal.

  ex A: 정말 고마워요. 길을 잘 알려 줘서 경복궁을 쉽게 찾았어요.
  B: 뭘요. 도움이 돼서 저도 기뻐요. /
  아니에요. 도움이 돼서 다행이에요. /
  별말씀을요. 모르는 게 있으면 언제든지 물어보세요.

Script

Zhang Souyi	Ichiro, I need to extend my visa. Do you know where I can do it?
Ichiro	You can do it at the immigration office. I extended mine there last week.
Zhang Souyi	Did you? So what do I need to get an extension?
Ichiro	You need your passport, certificate of alien registration, and a certificate of enrollment. You can apply for your certificate of enrollment at school.
Zhang Souyi	Okay, thanks. But can I fill out the application for a visa extension at the immigration office?
Ichiro	Of course. Also, you need to put your picture and a revenue stamp on the application.
Zhang Souyi	Wait a minute. I need to write it down. 'Stick my picture and a revenue stamp on the application.' But where do I buy the revenue stamp?
Ichiro	They sell it at the immigration office. When are you going to extend your visa?
Zhang Souyi	I'll go as soon as I get the certificate of enrollment from school. Thank you, Ichiro.
Ichiro	No problem. If you have any questions, ask me anytime.

Answers

(1) ③

Two people are talking about the place(the immigration office) to go to extend a visa and things that are needed to gain a visa extension.

(2) ③, ④

(3) ① 네 ② 네 ③ 아니요

You can extend your visa and buy a revenue stamp at the immigration office. Zhang Souyi is going to the immigration office as soon as she gets the certificate of enrollment that she applied for at school. But Zhang Souyi is not planning to go to the immigration office with Ichiro.

Vocabulary & Expression

소포를 저울 위에 올리세요

소포를 저울 위에 올리세요 means ***put the parcel on the scale please.*** When you put an object on something, you can say N을/를 N에 올리다.

ex 소포 무게를 재려면 소포를 저울 위에 올리세요.

ex 작은 짐을 큰 짐 위에 올리세요.

Functional Expression

- **Answering a question about the contents of a parcel**

  When you respond to a question about the contents of a parcel, you can say 내용물은 N예요/이에요, 안에 있는 건 N예요/이에요, 이 안에는 N이/가 들어 있어요, etc.

  ex A: 소포 안에 뭐가 있어요?
  B: (내용물은) 책이에요. /
  안에 있는 건 책이에요. /
  안에 든 건 책이에요. 무겁지는 않아요. /
  이 안에는 책이 들어 있어요. 가벼운 거예요.

- **Asking about the method of postage**

  At the post office, customers are asked how they want to send a parcel with expressions such as 어떻게 보내 드릴까요?, 무엇으로 보내시겠어요?, 어떤 방법으로 보낼까요?

  ex A: 이 소포를 어떻게 보내 드릴까요? /
  이 소포를 무엇으로 보내시겠어요? /
  이 소포를 어떤 방법으로 보낼까요?
  B: 배편으로 보낼게요.

Dialogue

Clerk	How are you? How may I help you?
Michael	I need to send a parcel to New York.
Clerk	Put your package on the scale please. (after a moment) It's 1.2 kg. What's inside? Anything fragile?
Michael	No, nothing fragile. It's a book.
Clerk	Would you like to send your parcel by airmail or by surface mail?
Michael	What is the rate?
Clerk	Airmail costs 38,400 won and surface mail costs 12,000 won.
Michael	How long does it take?
Clerk	It takes about 4-5 days by airmail and about a month by surface mail.
Michael	Then I'll send it by airmail. But can the parcel be delivered as soon as it arrives in New York?
Clerk	Yes. I'll put 'quick delivery' on it.
Michael	Thank you.

Grammar Focus

대신(에) is attached to a noun when the object assumes a job or role in place of another. 대신(에) is used whether the noun ends in a consonant or a vowel, and 에 can be omitted.

Noun	대신(에)	Noun	대신(에)
차	차 대신(에)	밥	밥 대신(에)
구두	구두 대신(에)	물	물 대신(에)
드라마	드라마 대신(에)	공책	공책 대신(에)
어머니	어머니 대신(에)	지하철	지하철 대신(에)

ex A: 음료수를 시킬까요?
B: 아니요. 저는 음료수 대신에 물을 마실게요.

ex A: 이치로 씨에게 문자 메시지를 보낼까요?
B: 문자 메시지 대신에 전화를 하는 게 어때요?

ex A: 아침에 보통 밥을 먹어요?
B: 아니요. 저는 아침에 시간이 없어서 밥 대신에 빵을 먹어요.

ex A: 살을 빼려면 어떻게 해야 돼요?
B: 그러면 엘리베이터 대신 계단을 이용하세요.

ex A: 오늘 등산 가야 하는데 등산화가 없어요.
B: 그럼 등산화 대신에 편한 운동화를 신으세요.

ex A: 오늘 율리아 씨 결혼식에 갈 거지요? 저도 갈 거예요.
B: 미안해요. 저는 오늘 시간이 없어요. 저 대신 마이클 씨가 가서 많이 축하해 주세요.

Answers

① A: 버스를 타고 왔어요?
B: 아니요. 길이 막혀서 버스 대신에 지하철을 타고 왔어요.

② A: 현금으로 계산했어요?
B: 아니요. 현금이 부족해서 현금 대신에 신용카드로 계산했어요.

③ A: 짐을 항공편으로 보냈어요?
B: 아니요. 너무 비싸서 항공편 대신에 배편으로 보냈어요.

④ A: 어제 친구와 뮤지컬을 봤어요?
B: 아니요. 표가 매진돼서 뮤지컬 대신에 영화를 봤어요.

⑤ A: 오늘 한국어 수업을 했어요?
B: 아니요. 문화 수업이 있어서 수업 대신에 공연 관람을 했어요.

Grammar Focus

-는 길에 is used to indicate that a person is on the way to a certain place or on the way back. It is used with a verb, usually one that represents movement such as 가다 or 오다. When a person is on the way at the very moment, -는 길이다 can be used.

Basic form	-는 길에	Basic form	-는 길에
가다	가는 길에	내려오다	내려오는 길에
오다	오는 길에	출근하다	출근하는 길에
돌아가다	돌아가는 길에	마중하다	마중하는 길에

ex A: 마이클 씨, 이번 방학 때 고향에 갈 거예요?
B: 네. 미국에 가는 길에 일본에도 잠깐 들를 거예요.

ex A: 언제 장소이 씨를 봤어요?
B: 집에 오는 길에 봤어요.

ex A: 나타샤 씨, 퇴근 후에 집으로 바로 갈 거예요?
B: 아니요. 퇴근하는 길에 슈퍼마켓에 들러서 요리 재료를 살 거예요.

ex A: 티엔 씨, 지금 어디에 가요?
B: 지금 학교에 가는 길이에요.

Focus Plus

- -는 길에 can be replaced with -는 도중에. However, -는 길에 can be used only with verbs representing movement such as 가다 or 오다, whereas -는 도중에 can be used with other verbs as well.

  ex 저녁 식사를 하는 도중에 뉴스를 봤다. (○)
  저녁 식사를 하는 길에 뉴스를 봤다. (×)

Answers

① A: 이치로 씨, 친구를 만났어요?
B: 네. 퇴근하는 길에 학교 앞에서 친구를 만났어요.

② A: 나타샤 씨, 두통약을 샀어요?
B: 네. 편의점에 가는 길에 약국에 들러서 두통약을 샀어요.

③ A: 얀 씨, 책을 반납했어요?
B: 네. 집으로 돌아오는 길에 도서관에 가서 책을 반납했어요.

④ A: 장소이 씨, 불꽃놀이를 봤어요?
B: 네. 어젯밤에 약속 장소로 가는 길에 불꽃놀이를 봤어요.

⑤ A: 왕카이 씨, 진찰을 받았어요?
B: 네. 기숙사로 돌아가는 길에 학교 보건소에서 진찰을 받았어요.

Grammar Focus

-다가 is used when a person stops what he/she is doing and does something else. The subject in the first clause is the same as that of the following clause. -다가 is attached to a verb and is used whether the verb stem ends in a consonant or a vowel. 가 can be omitted.

Basic form	-다가	Basic form	-다가
가다	가다가	돕다	돕다가
읽다	읽다가	듣다	듣다가
만들다	만들다가	짓다	짓다가

ex A: 어제 저녁에 그 드라마 봤어요?
B: 아니요. 보다가 잠이 들어서 끝까지 다 못 봤어요.

ex A: 요즘에도 태권도를 배워요?
B: 아니요. 너무 바빠서 배우다가 그만두었어요.

ex A: 음식을 왜 다 안 먹어요?
B: 배가 불러서 먹다가 남겼어요.

ex A: 학교까지 걸어서 왔어요?
B: 아니요. 걷다가 다리가 아파서 택시를 탔어요.

ex 수진 씨가 의자에 앉다가 넘어졌다. (○)
수진 씨가 의자에 앉다가 왕카이 씨가 넘어졌다. (×)

Focus Plus

- When a person stops in the middle of doing something, -다가 말다 is used. However, when two opposite actions are repeated in turn -다가 -다가 하다 can be used.

  ex A: 케이크를 다 만들었어요?
  B: 아니요. 시간이 없어서 만들다가 말았어요.

  ex A: 왜 그렇게 피곤해 보여요?
  B: 어젯밤에 잠을 잘 못 잤어요. 배가 아파서 자다가 깨다가 했어요.

Answers

① 티엔 씨는 자다가 무서운 꿈을 꿔서 잠에서 깼어요.
② 장소이 씨는 영화를 보다가 지루해서 중간에 나왔어요.
③ 미셸 씨는 학교에 가다가 숙제를 안 가져와서 집에 다시 가고 있어요.
④ 왕카이 씨는 예습을 하다가 어려운 단어가 있어서 사전을 찾고 있어요.
⑤ 나타샤 씨는 음식을 만들다가 재료가 모자라서 재료를 사러 갔어요.

Vocabulary & Expression

자료 검색

자료 검색 means ***searching for materials***. You can say 자료를 검색하다 when searching for materials that you need on the Internet, 클릭하다 when you click the mouse, and N(이)라고 치다 when you type in the search word. 화면에 N이/가 나오다 means that the Internet search has brought up the results on the screen.

ex A: 어떻게 하면 인터넷에서 비빔밥 만드는 방법을 찾을 수 있어요?
B: 인터넷 홈페이지에 '비빔밥 만들기'라고 쳐 보세요. 그러면 만드는 방법이 나올 거예요.

ex A: 방금 받은 메일을 확인하려면 어떻게 해야 해요?
B: 이메일 홈페이지를 열고 새로 온 이메일을 클릭하세요.

Script

Zhang Souyi	Excuse me, I need to search for some books about Korean pop music on the library website. Could you tell me how to do it?
Staff	Come this way. Let me help you as we look at the screen together. If you open this website right here, the book search function is at the top, right?
Zhang Souyi	Yes, there it is. What next?
Staff	Click the entire database in the book search and you'll see a box on the screen where you can input the names of the book and the author. In the title section, write the name of the book, and in the author section write the name of the writer.
Zhang Souyi	Can I write 'Korean pop music' instead of the name of the book?
Staff	Yes, if you do that, it will show all the books regarding Korean pop music that we have. Then, you can select the books you want there.
Zhang Souyi	Okay, I see. But where's the photocopy room in the library?
Staff	It's on the first floor. Find the book you want and you can make photocopies on the way down.
Zhang Souyi	Thank you very much.
Staff	No problem. If you have any questions when searching for the books, you can ask me again.

Answers

(1) ②
Zhang Souyi wants to find books on Korean pop music.

(2) ①

(3) ① 아니요 ② 아니요 ③ 네
Zhang Souyi is looking for books on Korean pop music without knowing any exact book titles. She is asking a library staff member for help since she does not know how to search for the relevant data.

Vocabulary & Expression

새로

새로 means ***anew, freshly***. It is used to indicate something that is new or done differently from before.

ex A: 집이 좀 달라진 것 같아요.
B: 작년에 집을 새로 고쳤어요.

ex A: 꽃병이 깨졌는데 어떻게 하지요?
B: 괜찮아요. 새로 사면 돼요.

네 자리

네 자리 means ***a four-digit number***. 자리 refers to how many digits there are in a number.

ex A: 카드 비밀번호 네 자리를 누르세요.
B: 네, 알겠습니다.

ex A: 여기 '010' 뒤에 전화번호 여덟 자리를 써 주세요.
B: 네, 알겠습니다.

Functional Expression

- **Expressing the purpose of a visit**

When you visit someone else's house or store with some specific purpose, you can explain the reason for your visit by saying –(으)러 왔는데요, –(으)려고 하는데요, or –아/어서 왔어요. Also, you can omit 왔는데요/왔어요 and just add 요 behind the reason or purpose.

ex A: 어서 오세요. 뭘 도와 드릴까요?
B: 현금 카드를 만들러 왔는데요. /
(= 만들러요)
현금 카드를 만들려고 하는데요. /
(= 만들려고요)
현금 카드를 만들고 싶어서 왔어요.
(= 만들고 싶어서요)

- **Asking whether one's card has been issued**

When you want to know if a card has been issued, you can say 카드가 나왔나요?, 카드 발급이 됐어요?, or 카드가 발급되었나요?

ex A: 카드가 나왔나요? /
카드 발급이 됐어요? /
카드가 발급되었나요? /
지금 카드 받을 수 있나요?
B: 네, 카드 여기 있습니다.

- **Answering questions about using a card**

  In response to someone asking from when a card can be used, you can use expressions such as 바로 사용하셔도 됩니다, 지금부터 쓰실 수 있습니다, and 바로 사용하실 수 있습니다.

  ex A: 이 카드 바로 쓸 수 있어요?
  B: 네, 바로 사용하셔도 됩니다. /
  네, 지금부터 쓰실 수 있습니다. /
  네, 바로 사용하실 수 있습니다.

- **Asking someone to input their password**

  When you ask someone to input his/her password, you can say 비밀번호를 누르세요, 비밀번호를 입력해 주세요, or 비밀번호 네 자리를 눌러 주세요.

  ex A: 비밀번호를 누르세요. /
  비밀번호를 입력해 주세요. /
  비밀번호 네 자리를 눌러 주세요.
  B: 네, 알겠습니다.

Dialogue

Bank clerk	How are you? How may I help you?
Zhang Souyi	I'd like to make a cash card.
Bank clerk	Well then, please write your name and address on this application.
Zhang Souyi	Alright. (after a while) I'm sorry but I made a mistake writing my address. What should I do?
Bank clerk	You can just write it again here. Do you have your seal with you?
Zhang Souyi	No, I don't.
Bank clerk	Then you can sign right here instead. Also, I need your ID.
Zhang Souyi	Yes, here you are. The application and my ID.
Bank clerk	Now press your four digit PIN number please. (after it's done) One more time please. (after a while) Your card is ready.
Zhang Souyi	Can I start using it today?
Bank clerk	Of course. You can use it right away, as soon as you get the card. You can try it at the ATM on your way out.
Zhang Souyi	Thank you.

Vocabulary & Expression

고민하다가

고민하다가 means ***after thinking about it for a while***. It suggests some action is taken 'after agonizing and thinking over a certain matter.' 고민하다 means worrying about something and thinking it over.

ex A: 이치로 씨, 그 일을 하기로 했군요.
B: 네, 오랫동안 고민하다가 하기로 결정했어요.

ex A: 미셸 씨, 무슨 고민이 있어요?
B: 네, 한국에서 취직하고 싶은데 어려울 것 같아서 고민이에요.

시계 바늘이 두 시 반을 가리키고 있었다

시계 바늘이 두 시 반을 가리키고 있었다 means ***the hands of the clock were pointing at 2:30***. It means that the time on the clock was 2:30. 가리키다 means that the fingers or some object are pointed in a certain direction or at a certain object to bring the fact to another person's attention.

ex A: 시계 바늘이 두 시 반을 가리키고 있어요.
B: 벌써 두 시 반이에요?

ex A: 지갑이 어디에 있어요? 저는 못 찾겠어요.
B: 저기 책상 아래에 있어요. 제가 손가락으로 가리키는 곳을 보세요.

ex A: 화장실이 어디에 있어요?
B: 저기에 가면 화살표가 있어요. 화살표가 가리키는 곳으로 가세요.

규칙을 어겨서

규칙을 어겨서 means ***since (I) broke the rules***. When you stick to the rules, you can say 규칙을 지키다, and when you don't, you can say 규칙을 어기다, 규칙을 깨다.

ex A: 어제 왜 기숙사 선생님께 혼이 났어요?
B: 방 안에서 요리를 했거든요. 규칙을 어겨서 야단맞았어요.

ex A: 수업 시간에 지켜야 하는 규칙에는 뭐가 있어요?
B: 수업 중에 휴대 전화를 사용하면 안 돼요.

ex A: 아이들이 교통 규칙을 잘 지키도록 가르쳐야 돼요.
B: 맞아요. 교통 규칙을 깨면 위험하잖아요.

Pronunciation

Double final consonants

When a syllable has two final consonants, it is said to have a double final consonant. When the final consonants are ㄳ, ㄵ, ㄶ, ㄽ, ㄾ, ㄼ, ㅀ, or ㅄ, the initial consonant should be pronounced. In the case of ㄺ, ㄻ, or ㄿ the final consonant should be pronounced. However, the final consonant in ㄺ should be pronounced as the first consonant [ㄹ] if ㄱ comes behind, as in -고.

ex 넓지[널찌], 앉기에는[안끼에는], 짧게[짤께], 여덟 시쯤[여덜씨쯤], 읽고[일꼬]

Text

A Sleepover with My Friends at the Dormitory

Last Friday, two of my friends from China came to Korea. It was really great to see them again after almost a year. For the first time in a long time the three of us had a delicious dinner together and did some shopping in Myeong-dong too. After looking around here and there, I was a bit tired and wanted to go in a coffee shop to chat and rest.

But my friends wanted to see my room instead of going to a coffee shop. We're not allowed to bring friends to our dormitory, but I really wanted to show them my room since they're such close friends. I thought about it for a while and finally ended up bringing my friends to my room.

My room is not big, but it was big enough for the three of us to sit in comfort. We ate some food they had brought from back home, and talked about our hometown as we looked at some photos. While we were chatting, we looked at the clock and saw that the hands were pointing at 2:30 am. The time had really gone fast. Ⓐ The next morning at around 8, we sneaked out of the dorm. Ⓑ I was worried since I had broken the rules, but it seemed like nobody saw us coming out so I was relieved. Ⓒ But when I came back from school and saw a memo posted on my room door, I freaked out. 'Wang Kai, come to the 1st floor office as soon as you get in.' I thought nobody had seen us. Ah, what should I do?

Answers

(1) ① 아니요 ② 네

(2) ①

While Wang Kai and his friends were chatting, it became 2 o'clock in the morning. So Wang Kai couldn't make his friends leave, considering they knew no Korean.

(3) **왕카이 씨는 기숙사의 규칙을 어기고 기숙사에서 친구들과 놀면서 같이 하룻밤을 보냈습니다. 그래서 사무실로부터 메모를 받았습니다.**

Vocabulary Check

▶ **Tick off the words and expressions that you know.**

우체국에서 / At the Post Office

- ☐ 무게를 달다 — to weigh
- ☐ 배달 소요 시간을 묻다 — to ask how long delivery will take
- ☐ 배달 요금을 내다 — to pay the postage fee
- ☐ 배편으로 보내다 — to send by surface mail
- ☐ 빠른우편으로 보내다 — to sent by express mail
- ☐ 소포 내용물을 묻다 — to ask about the contents of the parcel
- ☐ 소포 보내는 방법을 묻다 — to ask how the parcel should be sent
- ☐ 소포를 포장하다 — to wrap a package
- ☐ 우표를 붙이다 — to put a stamp on
- ☐ 인편으로 보내다 — to send by personal delivery
- ☐ 저울에 올리다 — to place on the scale
- ☐ 주소를 적다 — to write down the address
- ☐ 편지를 배달하다 — to deliver a letter
- ☐ 항공편으로 보내다 — to send by air mail

출입국관리사무소에서 / At the Immigration Office

- ☐ 비자를 받다 — to receive a visa
- ☐ 비자를 연장하다 — to extend a visa
- ☐ 비자 연장 신청서를 쓰다 — to write the application for a visa extension
- ☐ 수입 인지를 사다 — to buy the revenue stamp
- ☐ 신청서에 사진을 붙이다 — to stick the photo on the application
- ☐ 신청서에 수입 인지를 붙이다 — to stick the revenue stamp on the application
- ☐ 외국인등록증을 내다 — to give one's alien registration card
- ☐ 재학증명서를 내다 — to give one's certificate of enrollment

은행에서 / At the Bank

- ☐ 계좌 번호를 알다 — to know one's account number
- ☐ 도장을 찍다 — to stamp one's seal
- ☐ 서명을 하다 — to sign one's name
- ☐ 신분증을 내다 — to give one's ID
- ☐ 신청서를 쓰다 — to fill out an application
- ☐ 운전면허증을 내다 — to give one's driver's license
- ☐ 카드를 발급하다 — to issue a card
- ☐ 통장을 만들다 — to open an account
- ☐ 학생증을 내다 — to give one's student ID
- ☐ 현금 인출기에서 확인하다 — to check at the ATM
- ☐ 현금 카드를 만들다 — to make a cash card

도서관에서 / At the Library

- ☐ 숙제를 하다 — to do homework
- ☐ 자료를 복사하다 — to photocopy materials
- ☐ 자료를 찾다 — to search for materials
- ☐ 저자를 검색하다 — to search the author's name
- ☐ 책을 검색하다 — to do a book search (online)
- ☐ 책을 반납하다 — to return a book
- ☐ 책을 빌리다 — to borrow a book
- ☐ 책을 읽다 — to read a book
- ☐ 홈페이지에 서명을 치다 — to input a name on the homepage
- ☐ 홈페이지에서 자료를 다운받다 — to download materials from the homepage

PART1 준비합시다 01 • –(으)ㅁ

p.74

Grammar Focus

–(으)ㅁ is used to end a sentence that briefly describes or notifies a fact in a notice, bulletin board, or memo. –았/었음 is used for a past fact and –(으)ㄹ 것임 is used for a future fact. It is attached to both verbs and adjectives.

Basic form	–(으)ㅁ	–았/었음	–(으)ㄹ 것임
바쁘다	바쁨	바빴음	–
작다	작음	작았음	–
만나다	만남	만났음	만날 것임
찾다	찾음	찾았음	찾을 것임
듣다	들음	들었음	들을 것임
돕다	도움	도왔음	도울 것임

ex "수요일에 문화 수업이 있어요." → 수요일에 문화 수업이 있음.

ex "이번 시험은 좀 어렵습니다." → 이번 시험은 좀 어려움.

ex "내일 약속이 토요일로 연기되었어요." → 내일 약속이 토요일로 연기되었음.

ex "내년에 고향에 집을 지을 거예요." → 내년에 고향에 집을 지을 것임.

Focus Plus

- –(으)ㅁ and –(으)ㄹ 것 are not for colloquial use but are used to write briefly in a memo or bulletin board. –(으)ㄹ 것 is used when taking a memo of directions ending in –(으)세요 or –(으)십시오. –(으)ㅁ is used in all other cases.

  ex "내일까지 밀린 숙제를 꼭 내세요."
  → 내일까지 밀린 숙제를 꼭 낼 것.

  "내일까지 밀린 숙제를 꼭 내야 합니다."
  → 내일까지 밀린 숙제를 꼭 내야 함.

- In ㄹ eliminated verbs such as 살다, 만들다, 놀다, 열다, 멀다, –(으)ㅁ is written as 삶, 만듦, 놂, 엶, and 멂.

  ex "오늘 요리 시간에 비빔밥을 만들어요."
  → 오늘 요리 시간에 비빔밥을 만듦.

Answers

① 전화한 사람: 티엔
내용: 오늘 학교에 오는 길에 교통사고가 났어요. 병원에 가야 해서 좀 늦을 것 같음.

② 전화한 사람: 이화여행사
내용: 다음 주 토요일에 갈 제주도 여행 예약을 확인하려고 전화했음.

③ 전화한 사람: 왕카이
내용: 다음 주에 미셸 씨 생일 파티가 있음. 생일 음식은 미셸 씨 집에서 친구들과 같이 만듦. 같이 가면 좋겠음.

Grammar Focus

–기(를) 바라다 is used to express that one wants a thing or situation to occur in a certain way. It is attached to both verbs and adjectives.

Basic form	–기(를) 바라다	Basic form	–기(를) 바라다
건강하다	건강하기를 바라다	만들다	만들기를 바라다
행운이 있다	행운이 있기를 바라다	돕다	돕기를 바라다
가다	가기를 바라다	듣다	듣기를 바라다
읽다	읽기를 바라다	짓다	짓기를 바라다

ex (카드에)
얀 씨, 이번 입사 시험에 꼭 합격하기를 바랍니다.

ex (초대장에)
나타샤 씨, 다음 주 금요일에 제 생일 파티를 합니다. 나타샤 씨가 꼭 제 생일 파티에 참석해 주시기를 바랍니다.

ex A: 수잔 씨, 결혼을 축하해요. 늘 행복하시기 바랍니다.
B: 네, 감사합니다.

ex A: 이치로 씨, 즐거운 연말연시를 보내시기 바랄게요.
B: 고마워요. 티엔 씨도 즐겁게 보내세요.

Focus Plus

- –았/었으면 하고 바라다 can replace –기(를) 바라다 to express the same meaning. While –기(를) 바라다 is usually used in a literary context or formal conversation, –았/었으면 하고 바라다 is used in everyday speech.

ex A: 6급까지 공부한 후에는 어떤 계획이 있어요?
B: 한국 회사에 취직했으면 하고 바라고 있어요.

Answers

① A: 친구가 내일 결혼을 해서 축하 카드를 쓰려고 해요. 카드에 어떻게 쓰면 좋을까요?
B: '행복하게 잘 살기를 바랍니다.'라고 쓰세요.

② A: 친구가 새로 커피숍을 열어서 축하 카드를 쓰려고 해요. 카드에 어떻게 쓰면 좋을까요?
B: '사업이 잘되기를 바랍니다.'라고 쓰세요.

③ A: 친구 할아버지의 환갑잔치가 있어서 축하 카드를 쓰려고 해요. 카드에 어떻게 쓰면 좋을까요?
B: '건강하게 오래 사시기를 바랍니다.'라고 쓰세요.

④ A: 친구가 내일 대학 입학시험을 봐서 응원 카드를 쓰려고 해요. 카드에 어떻게 쓰면 좋을까요?
B: '꼭 가고 싶은 대학에 합격하기를 바랍니다.'라고 쓰세요.

⑤ A: 친구가 병원에 입원해서 병문안을 가려고 해요. 카드에 어떻게 쓰면 좋을까요?
B: '빨리 회복되기를 바랍니다.'라고 쓰세요.

Vocabulary & Expression

수저를 들고

수저를 들고 means ***lifting a spoon or a spoon and chopsticks***. 들다 means to lift something, or move something from a lower position to an upper position. Therefore, 수저를 들다 means lifting with the hands a spoon or a spoon and chopsticks from a lower place such as a table.

ex A: 마이클 씨, 잠깐만요. 할아버지와 식사를 할 때는 어른이 먼저 수저를 드신 후에 식사를 시작해야 합니다.
B: 아, 그래요? 죄송합니다.

ex A: 우리 민호 친구들이 많이 와서 기뻐요. 어서 먹읍시다.
B: 할머니, 먼저 수저를 드시지요. 그러면 저희도 먹기 시작하겠습니다.

ex A: 지난 토요일에 마라톤 했지요? 많이 힘들었어요?
B: 네, 너무 힘들어서 밥 먹을 때 수저를 들 힘도 없었어요.

입을 필요는 없어요

입을 필요는 없다 means ***that (you) don't have to wear it***. It indicates that one doesn't have to wear something. In other words, one may choose whether to wear it or not.

ex A: 등산 갈 때 꼭 등산복을 입어야 돼요?
B: 등산복을 꼭 입을 필요는 없어요. 편한 옷이면 돼요.

ex A: 내일 회사 면접시험을 보러 가는데 꼭 치마를 입어야 할까요?
B: 꼭 치마를 입을 필요 없어요. 단정하게 재킷에 바지를 입고 가도 돼요.

ex A: 이 책을 도서관에 오늘 꼭 반납해야 돼요?
B: 오늘 꼭 할 필요는 없어요. 이번 주 금요일까지 하면 돼요.

맨발

맨발 means ***barefoot***. It indicates that the feet are bare, without any socks or shoes.

ex A: 나타샤 씨, 수업 후에 집에 돌아가면 아이가 무척 반가워하죠?
B: 그럼요. 제 얼굴을 보면 맨발로 뛰어나와서 저를 안아요.

ex A: 다른 사람 집에 갈 때 양말 안 신고 맨발로 가도 돼요?
B: 어른이 계신 집에는 그렇게 가면 실례가 될 수 있어요.

ex A: 우리 내일 해수욕 가죠? 수잔 씨는 운동화를 가져갈 거예요?
B: 아니요. 그냥 맨발에 샌들 신고 갈 거예요.

Functional Expression

- **Telling someone to have a good time at a friend's house.**

When a friend is visiting another friend's house and you want to express your hopes that he/she has a good time, you can say 즐겁게 보내고 오세요, 즐겁게 보내기를 바랄게요, or 재미있게 놀고 왔으면 해요.

ex A: 친구 집에서 즐겁게 보내고 오세요. /
친구 집에 가서 즐겁게 보내기를 바랄게요. /
친구 집에 가서 재미있게 놀고 왔으면 해요.
B: 네, 고마워요.

Script

Ichiro	Junyeong, I've been invited to my Korean friend's house but I've never visited a house where the grandparents live also. So I want to ask you a few things.
Han Junyeong	Sure. What do you want to know?
Ichiro	Are there any particular table manners?
Han Junyeong	Yeah, you shouldn't lift your spoon before the grandparents do. You can start eating after they have started. Don't eat with your bowl of soup or rice in your hands. Your bowls should be on the table while you eat.
Ichiro	I see. What should I wear? Do I have to wear a suit?
Han Junyeong	You don't have to wear a suit. You can wear something neat and clean. Just don't go barefoot or wear shorts. It can be considered rude.
Ichiro	What kind of present should I take for the grandparents?
Han Junyeong	Well, we usually take fruit or drinks. But you should first ask your friend what they like.
Ichiro	All right. Thank you for your advice.
Han Junyeong	My pleasure. I hope you have a good time at your friend's house.

Answers

(1) ① 아니요 ② 네

At mealtimes, people start eating only after their grandparents have started. In Korea, people do not eat with their bowls of rice or soup in their hands. Instead, the bowls should stay on the table while eating.

(2) ②

Since the grandparents also live in Ichiro's friend's house, wearing shorts or sandals or going barefoot is not appropriate.

(3) ②

Ichiro will ask his friend what kind of present he should take for the grandparents.

Vocabulary & Expression

급한 일

급한 일 means ***urgent business***. 급하다 means that something has to be done in a hurry because there is little time.

ex A: 마이클 씨, 어제 왜 우리 반 모임에 안 왔어요? 다들 기다렸어요.
B: 죄송해요. 회사에 급한 일이 생겨서 못 갔어요.

Functional Expression

- **Asking if there is any message to leave**

You've picked up the phone for another person but he/she is not there. To ask the person on the phone if he/she wants to leave a message, you can say 전하실 말씀이 있어요?, 전해 드릴 말씀이 있으세요? or 전하고 싶은 말씀이 있으세요?

ex A: 전하실 말씀이 있어요? / 전해 드릴 말씀이 있으세요? / 전하고 싶은 말씀이 있으세요?
B: 네. 메모 좀 부탁드립니다.

Dialogue

Gang Hoyeong	Hello? May I speak to Wang Kai?
Ichiro	He's not here right now. He's gone out.
Gang Hoyeong	I'm sorry but do you know when he's coming back?
Ichiro	Well, I am not sure. Would you like to leave a message?
Gang Hoyeong	Yes, this is Gang Hoyeong speaking, Wang Kai's friend from his club. Can I leave a message for him?
Ichiro	Sure, hold on please. Okay, go ahead.
Gang Hoyeong	I called him about the date he's supposed to visit my house. He was going to come this Saturday, but something urgent came up. So I want to ask him if he can visit me next Saturday instead.
Ichiro	All right. Who's speaking again?
Gang Hoyeong	This is Gang Hoyeong speaking. Please give him my message.
Ichiro	Sure, I will.

To Wang Kai,
– Gang Hoyeong, a friend from your club, called.
– He called to discuss the date you are supposed to visit his house.
– Gang Hoyeong has something urgent to do this Saturday.
– He called to postpone your visit to next Saturday.

Ichiro, 4:00 p.m.

Grammar Focus

아무 is used to show that everything is possible without making any particular choice. 아무나 is used to refer to any person, 아무거나 is used for anything, and 아무 데나 is used to indicate any direction or destination of movement. 아무 때나 is used to indicate that something can be done at any time, while 아무 데서나 is used to indicate that something can be done anywhere.

누구?	아무나	어디에?	아무 데나
무엇?	아무거나	어디에서?	아무 데서나
언제?	아무 때나	누구에게?	아무에게나

ex A: 수잔 씨하고 티엔 씨 중에서 누구하고 같이 일하고 싶어요?
B: 둘 다 일을 열심히 하니까 아무나 괜찮아요.

ex A: 점심에 뭘 먹을까요? 피자, 비빔밥, 스파게티 중에서 어떤 게 좋아요?
B: 다 제가 좋아하는 거예요. 아무거나 다 괜찮아요.

ex A: 선생님, 언제 전화 드리면 돼요?
B: 저녁 9시 전이면 아무 때나 괜찮아요. 편한 시간에 전화 주세요.

ex A: 이번 휴가에 경주에 갈까요, 부산에 갈까요?
B: 저는 아무 데나 괜찮아요. 둘 다 안 가 봤어요.

ex A: 학교 도서관에 아무나 들어갈 수 있어요?
B: 아니요. 학생증이 있어야 돼요. 아무나 들어갈 수 없어요.

ex A: 왕카이 씨, 이 공항에서는 아무 데서나 담배를 피우면 안 돼요. 저쪽에 있는 흡연실에서만 돼요.
B: 그래요? 죄송해요.

Answers

① A: 수업 후에 뭘 먹고 싶어요? 비빔밥을 먹을까요, 아니면 피자를 먹을까요?
B: 너무 배가 고프니까 저는 아무거나 다 괜찮아요.

② A: 언제 만나고 싶어요? 평일에 만날까요, 아니면 주말에 만날까요?
B: 중요한 약속이 없으니까 저는 아무 때나 다 괜찮아요.

③ A: 누구와 영화를 같이 보고 싶어요? 장소이 씨와 볼까요, 아니면 티엔 씨와 볼까요?
B: 둘 다 친한 사람들이니까 저는 아무나/아무하고나 다 괜찮아요.

④ A: 어디에서 쇼핑하고 싶어요? 남대문 시장에서 쇼핑할까요, 아니면 이태원에서 쇼핑할까요?
B: 두 곳 다 예쁘고 싼 옷이 많으니까 저는 아무 데나/아무 데서나 다 괜찮아요.

⑤ A: 비행기에서 어디에 앉고 싶어요? 창가 자리에 앉을래요, 아니면 통로 자리에 앉을래요?
B: 비행 시간이 짧으니까 저는 아무 데나 다 괜찮아요.

Grammar Focus

–잖아요 is used to confirm what the listener or other people already know or to correct or inform the listener who doesn't remember or know the situation. –았/었잖아요 is used for a past fact and –(으)ㄹ 거잖아요 is used for a future fact.

Basic form	–잖아요	Basic form	–잖아요
싸다	싸잖아요	가다	가잖아요
작다	작잖아요	먹다	먹잖아요
맛있다	맛있잖아요	학생이다	학생이잖아요

ex A: 진차오 씨하고 같이 점심 먹을 건데 김치볶음밥 어떨까요?
B: 안 돼요. 진차오 씨는 매운 거 안 좋아하잖아요.

ex A: 요즘 친구들을 전혀 만날 수 없어요. 다들 무슨 일이 있나요?
B: 무슨 일은요. 지난주에는 시험 때문에 모두 바빴잖아요.

ex A: 선생님, 여행도 가고 친구들하고도 놀고 싶은데 공부 때문에 너무 바쁘고 힘들어요.
B: 내년 2월이면 곧 대학교 졸업할 거잖아요. 졸업한 후에 신나게 노세요.

Focus Plus

- –잖아요 is generally used with friends or other people one is close to or with people who are younger or in a lower position.

ex (회사에서)
A: 김민호 씨, 이 일을 오늘까지 하기로 하지 않았어요?
B: 부장님, 죄송합니다. 다른 급한 일이 있어서 못 했습니다. (○)
부장님, 죄송합니다. 다른 급한 일이 있었잖아요. 그래서 못 했습니다. (×)

Answers

① A: 미셸 씨에게 어떤 선물을 주면 좋을까요? 케이크는 어때요?
B: 케이크보다 과일을 선물하는 게 좋겠어요. 미셸 씨가 케이크를 안 좋아하잖아요.
A: 그럼 과일을 선물하기로 해요.

② A: 나타샤 씨에게 어떤 선물을 주면 좋을까요? 귀걸이는 어때요?
B: 귀걸이보다 손수건을 선물하는 게 좋겠어요. 나타샤 씨가 좋아하는 취향을 모르잖아요.
A: 그럼 손수건을 선물하기로 해요.

③ A: 티엔 씨에게 어떤 선물을 주면 좋을까요? 구두는 어때요?
B: 구두보다 운동화 선물하는 게 좋겠어요. 티엔 씨는 평소에 캐주얼을 즐겨 입잖아요.
A: 그럼 운동화를 선물하기로 해요.

④ A: 율리아 씨에게 어떤 선물을 주면 좋을까요? 향수는 어때요?
B: 향수보다 화장품을 선물하는 게 좋겠어요. 율리아 씨는 향수를 별로 사용하지 않잖아요.
A: 그럼 화장품을 선물하기로 해요.

⑤ A: 왕카이 씨에게 어떤 선물을 주면 좋을까요? 전자사전은 어때요?
B: 전자사전보다 MP3를 선물하는 게 좋겠어요. 왕카이 씨는 얼마 전에 전자사전을 샀잖아요.
A: 그럼 MP3를 선물하기로 해요.

Grammar Focus

-(으)ㄴ/는데요 is used when one anticipates the listener's reaction while presenting a situation related or contradictory to what one is planning to say. Adjectives combine with -(으)ㄴ데요 for present facts, verbs are used with -는데요 for present facts, and both adjectives and verbs are used with -았/었는데요 for past facts. Verbs are used with -(으)ㄹ 건데요 for future facts.

Basic form	-았/었는데요	-(으)ㄴ/는데요	-(으)ㄹ 건데요
예쁘다	예뻤는데요	예쁜데요	-
많다	많았는데요	많은데요	-
멀다	멀었는데요	먼데요	-
어렵다	어려웠는데요	어려운데요	-
가다	갔는데요	가는데요	갈 건데요
먹다	먹었는데요	먹는데요	먹을 건데요
만들다	만들었는데요	만드는데요	만들 건데요
짓다	지었는데요	짓는데요	지을 건데요

ex A: 여보세요. 마이클 씨 좀 부탁합니다.
B: 지금 자리에 안 계신데요.

ex A: 장소이 씨, 지금 어디에서 살아요?
B: 학교 근처에서 사는데요. 아주 깨끗하고 좋아요.

ex A: 이번 주에 시작한 영화를 같이 볼래요?
B: 전 그 영화 벌써 봤는데요.

ex A: 선생님, 내년에 대학 입학시험을 볼 건데요. 뭘 준비하면 좋을까요?
B: 우선 한국어 공부를 열심히 할 필요가 있어요.

Answers

① A: 버스를 타고 갈래요?
B: 지금 길이 많이 막히는데요.
A: 그래요? 그럼 지하철을 타고 갑시다.

② A: 나가서 산책할래요?
B: 밖에 날씨가 쌀쌀한데요.
A: 그래요? 그럼 집에서 텔레비전이나 봅시다.

③ A: 이 서류를 검토해 줄래요?
B: 방금 사장님이 부르셨는데요.
A: 그래요? 그럼 사장님을 뵙고 나서 이야기합시다.

④ A: 점심에 음식을 배달시킬래요?
B: 회의 시간이 30분밖에 안 남았는데요.
A: 그래요? 그럼 편의점에서 간단한 걸 사 먹읍시다.

Vocabulary & Expression

어쩐 일이에요?

어쩐 일이에요? means ***what is the matter?*** 어쩐 일 indicates a certain matter or a reason. Therefore, 어쩐 일이에요? is a way of asking what the matter is or asking a person the reason he/she does something. You can also say 무슨 일이에요? or 웬일이에요?

ex A: 수잔 씨, 이 시간에 어쩐 일이에요?
B: 근처에 왔는데 티엔 씨 생각이 나서 잠깐 들렀어요.

ex A: 마이클 씨, 전화하셨죠? 무슨 일이에요?
B: 내일 말하기 시험이 있어요. 마이클 씨가 오늘 결석해서 알려 주려고요.

ex A: 왕카이 씨, 웬일이에요? 무슨 일로 양복을 입고 학교에 왔어요?
B: 수업 끝나고 바로 친구 결혼식에 가야 해서 입고 왔어요.

집들이

집들이 means ***housewarming party***. It is a party where you invite friends or neighbors to your new house to share a meal and look around the house.

ex A: 얀 씨, 집들이가 언제였죠?
B: 다음 주 금요일요. 시간 괜찮으시죠?

ex A: 지난번 왕카이 씨 집들이 때 진차오 씨는 왜 안 왔어요?
B: 그때 감기 때문에 못 갔어요. 저는 그 다음 주에 왕카이 씨 집에 가서 집구경도 하고 재미있게 놀고 왔어요.

ex A: 수잔 씨, 요즘 집들이 때문에 스트레스를 받아요.
B: 나타샤 씨, 너무 스트레스 받지 마세요. 잘할 수 있는 거 두세 개만 해도 돼요.

진수성찬

진수성찬 means a ***sumptuous feast/spread***. It means a specially prepared meal that is abundant and delicious.

ex A: 얀 씨, 집들이 음식이 너무 많네요. 진수성찬이에요.
B: 입에 맞으면 좋겠어요. 맛있게 드세요.

ex A: 작년에 일본에 있는 친구 집에 놀러 갔는데 친구 어머니가 생선에 고기, 야채까지 진수성찬을 차려 주셨어요.
B: 정말 맛있게 먹었겠네요.

ex A: 우와, 진수성찬이네요.
B: 나타샤 씨, 언제나 이렇게 진수성찬을 드세요?
A: 아니에요. 오늘 장소이 씨가 와서 잘하는 걸로 몇 개 해 봤어요.

Functional Expression

- **Saying that a lot of delicious things to eat have been prepared**

When it is evident that a lot of delicious food has been prepared for a meal you can say 진수성찬이에요, 음식이 없는 게 없네요 or 상다리가 부러지겠어요.

ex A: 진수성찬이에요. /
음식이 없는 게 없네요. /
음식이 너무 많아서 상다리가 부러지겠어요.
B: 맛있게 드세요.

Script

Eungyeong Natasha, come on in! What's up?

Natasha Hello, Eungyeong. I came to ask you something. We're having a house-warming party next Friday but I'm not good at making Korean food. What kind of food should I prepare?

Eungyeong Well, *bulgogi* or *japchae* are quite common for a party. You can also make *hobak jeon* (battered and pan-fried zucchini) or *sogogi jeon* (battered and pan-fried beef).

Natasha I have made *bulgogi* before so I guess I can make that. But I have never made *japchae*.

Eungyeong It's not so hard to make *japchae*. You can make it with some help from a cookbook. I will lend you my cookbook.

Natasha Wow, thank you. How about dessert?

Eungyeong Anything like a cake or fruit will do. Oh, you're good at making cakes, aren't you? Your party will be as good as a feast with *bulgogi*, *japchae* and a cake!

Answers

(1) ③
Natasha is asking Eungyeong what she should prepare for her housewarming party.

(2) **잡채, 불고기, 케이크**
Natasha is planning to make *bulgogi*, which she has made before, *japchae*, which is not so hard to cook, and a cake, which she is good at making.

(3) ① 네 ② 네 ③ 아니요
For dessert, both fruit and a cake are good options. Eungyeong will not help Natasha prepare the meal but will lend Natasha her cookbook.

Vocabulary & Expression

부엌용품이나 생활용품

부엌용품이나 생활용품 means ***kitchen utensils or daily supplies.*** 부엌용품 means a utensil used in cooking and 생활용품 means an item necessary for daily life such as toilet paper or lotion.

ex A: 부엌용품에는 뭐가 있어요?
B: 냄비, 프라이팬, 컵, 그릇 같은 게 있어요.

ex A: 집들이 선물로 부엌용품이나 생활용품 어때요?
B: 로션이나 화장지 같은 생활용품이 좋겠어요.

기억에도 남을 것 같은데요

기억에 남을 것 같은데요 means ***it will remain in (my) memory.*** 기억에 남다 means previous impressions or experiences remain in one's memory without being forgotten.

ex A: 어제 본 영화 장면 중에서 뭐가 가장 좋았어요?
B: 두 사람이 바닷가에서 만나는 장면이 너무 멋있었어요. 오랫동안 기억에 남을 것 같아요.

Functional Expression

- **Saying that you can be reached on the phone at anytime**

  You can say 아무 때나 괜찮아요, 언제나 시간이 돼요, or 바쁘지 않아요. 언제든지 좋아요 when you are available to talk on the phone at anytime.

  ex A: 언제 전화 드릴까요?
  B: 저는 아무 때나 괜찮으니까 전화 주세요. /
  언제나 시간이 되니까 편한 시간에 전화 주세요. /
  요즘 바쁘지 않아요. 언제든지 좋아요. 전화하세요.

Dialogue

Zhang Souyi	Michelle, you know there is a housewarming party at Natasha's next Wednesday. What should I get for a present?
Michelle	You're right. What would make a good present?
Zhang Souyi	In Korea, people usually give kitchen utensils or everyday goods when they're invited to a housewarming party. How about laundry detergent or toilet paper?
Michelle	They're okay but I don't want to give something anyone can give. I'd like to get her something special.
Zhang Souyi	You're right. Then what should we get?
Michelle	How about a coffee cup?
Zhang Souyi	A coffee cup?
Michelle	We can have a photo or message imprinted on a coffee cup. How about a set of coffee cups with a photo of our classmates on them?
Zhang Souyi	That's a good idea. Then do you want to meet this weekend to go and buy them?
Michelle	Sure. I'm free anytime on the weekend, so give me a call.

Vocabulary & Expression

새 학기를 맞아서

새 학기를 맞아서 means ***starting a new school term.*** 새 학기 means a new school term and 맞다 means that one confronts/deals with a certain occasion when time has passed. 맞다 can be used in expressions such as 봄을 맞다, 새해를 맞다, 추석을 맞다 or 생일을 맞다.

ex A: 노래 동아리에서 개강 모임을 해요?
B: 네, 새 학기를 맞아서 모임을 하기로 했어요.

ex A: 이번 달에 생일을 맞은 사람이 누구예요?
B: 티엔 씨하고 수잔 씨예요.

ex A: 백화점에서 추석을 맞아서 바겐세일을 크게 해요.
B: 정말요? 살 게 있었는데 가 봐야겠어요.

Functional Expression

- **Saying that it's been a while**

You can say 한동안 연락하지 못했네요, 오랫동안 소식을 몰랐지요? or 그동안 연락이 끊겨서 서로 소식을 못 전했어요 when you meet someone you've lost touch with for a while.

ex A: 우리 한동안 연락하지 못했네요. /
우리 서로 바빠서 오랫동안 소식을 몰랐지요? /
우리 그동안 연락이 끊겨서 소식을 못 전했어요.
B: 그러게요. 반가워요. 그동안 어떻게 지냈어요?

Text

Title: [FW] Get-together of the Chinese-learning club for the new semester
Sent: Park Hyeonmi 〈apple@ewha.ac.kr〉

Dear Zhang Souyi,
Hello, Zhang Souyi. This is Park Hyeonmi.
How have you been? I haven't been in touch with you for a while as I've been busy preparing for the new school term. There is a get-together of the Chinese-learning club to celebrate the beginning of the new term this Friday. We are inviting our Chinese friends this time so I would like to invite you. It will be held in a restaurant named Circle in front of the school on Friday, October 6. Can you join us, Zhang Souyi? Let's have some delicious food and a nice talk. I am forwarding the invitation from the club, so please take a look and join us if you are free.
I want to send an invitation to Wang Kai too but I don't have his contact information. Do you have it? You guys are close friends, right? If you have his contact details, please let me know. I look forward to your reply.

Title: Get-together of the Chinese-learning club for the new semester
Sent: Park Heejun 〈park@ewha.ac.kr〉

Hello, everyone in the Chinese-learning club!
We are going to have a get-together as the new school term has started. But this time we are going to invite our Chinese friends. We want it to be an occasion where we talk and learn about each other's culture while eating the traditional food of both Korea and China. If you don't have a Chinese friend, you can come alone! Please come and join us!
– Date: October 6 (Friday), 6:00 pm
– Place: Circle, in front of school (Food will be prepared by the restaurant)
– Dues: 20,000 won (No dues for Chinese friends)
– Bring: A gift under 5,000 won

Best regards,

Park Heejun
President of the Chinese-learning club

Pronunciation

Nasal sound

The final consonant sound [ㄷ] is pronounced [ㄴ] before ㄴ or ㅁ.

ex 못했네요[모탠네요], 있는데요[인는데요], 맛있는[마신는], 있나요[인나요]

Answers

(1) ③
Park Hyeonmi is inviting Zhang Souyi to a get-together of the club to celebrate the beginning of a new school term.

(2) ① 아니요 ② 아니요 ③ 네
Foreigners are not always invited to the meeting, but just to this get-together for the beginning of the new school term. Also, anyone who doesn't have a Chinese friend can still come alone. Park Hyeonmi also wanted to send an invitation to Wang Kai but she couldn't because she didn't have his contact details.

(3) **② 중국인 친구를 초대해서 동아리 모임에 갔습니다.**
People are preparing food in ①. Since food will be prepared by the restaurant, there is no need to bring food. Also, the price of the present in ③ is 20,000 won. However, a gift worth under 5,000 won has to be prepared.

Vocabulary Check

▶ **Tick off the words and expressions that you know.**

초대	Invitation
☐ 감사장을 쓰다	to write a thank-you letter
☐ 선물을 상의하다	to ask one's advice about a gift
☐ 손님을 대접하다	to entertain one's guests
☐ 손님을 마중하다	to greet one's guests
☐ 손님을 배웅하다	to see off one's guests
☐ 약속 날짜를 바꾸다	to change the appointment date
☐ 약속 시간을 변경하다	to change the appointment time
☐ 약속을 연기하다	to postpone an appointment
☐ 음식을 차리다	to set the table
☐ 장을 보다	to go shopping
☐ 집들이를 하다	to have a housewarming party
☐ 집을 방문하다	to visit one's house
☐ 초대장을 쓰다	to write an invitation

축하	Celebration
☐ 결혼하다	to marry
☐ 대학교에 입학하다 / 진학하다	to enter university
☐ 병이 회복되다	to recover from illness
☐ 사업을 시작하다	to start one's own business
☐ 사업이 잘 되다	to do well in business
☐ 새 집으로 이사를 하다	to move to a new house
☐ 시험에 합격하다	to pass an exam
☐ 아기가 태어나다	to have a baby born
☐ 장학금을 받다	to receive a scholarship
☐ 학교를 졸업하다	to graduate from school
☐ 회사에 취직하다	to get a job in a company
☐ 회사에서 승진하다	to get promoted at work

집들이 선물	Housewarming Gifts
☐ 가루비누	washing powder (laundry detergent)
☐ 목욕용품	bath goods
☐ 부엌용품	kitchen ware
☐ 생활용품	everyday goods
☐ 성냥	matches
☐ 세탁세제	laundry detergent
☐ 커피 잔	coffee cup
☐ 포도주	wine
☐ 휴지	tissues

PART1 준비합시다 01 • -(으)ㄴ/는지 알다

p.92

Grammar Focus

-(으)ㄴ/는지 알다 is used to indicate that one is aware of a certain fact. It is attached to an adjective or a verb. -은지 is used if the stem of the adjective ends in a consonant, while -ㄴ지 is used if it ends in a vowel or the consonant ㄹ. In the case of verbs, -는지 is used whether the verb stem ends in a consonant or a vowel. -았/었는지 is used with past tense verbs and -(으)ㄹ 건지 is used with future tense verbs. When a person does not know a certain fact, you can use -(으)ㄴ/는지 모르다. It is often used with interrogative pronouns such as 언제, 누구, 무엇, 왜, and 얼마나.

Basic form	-(으)ㄴ지	-았/었는지	Basic form	-는지	-았/었는지	-(으)ㄹ 건지
싸다	싼지	쌌는지	오다	오는지	왔는지	올 건지
크다	큰지	컸는지	입다	입는지	입었는지	입을 건지
작다	작은지	작았는지	듣다	듣는지	들었는지	들을 건지
멀다	먼지	멀었는지	팔다	파는지	팔았는지	팔 건지
덥다	더운지	더웠는지	돕다	돕는지	도왔는지	도울 건지
그렇다	그런지	그랬는지	짓다	짓는지	지었는지	지을 건지

ex A: 학교 앞에 사람들이 왜 많은지 알아요?
B: 네. 학교 앞에서 드라마를 찍고 있어서 사람들이 많아요.

ex A: 영화가 몇 시에 시작하는지 알아요?
B: 아니요, 언제 시작하는지 몰라요.

ex A: 나타샤 씨가 왜 한국에서 살았는지 알아요?
B: 네. 나타샤 씨 남편이 한국에서 일해서 한국에서 살았어요.

ex A: 한준영 씨의 생일이 언제인지 알아요?
B: 아니요, 몰라요.

Answers

① A: 서울 시청에서 인천공항까지 얼마나 걸리는지 압니까?
B: 네, 얼마나 걸리는지 알아요.

② A: 한글을 누가 만들었는지 압니까?
B: 네, 누가 만들었는지 알아요.

③ A: KTX가 얼마나 빠른지 압니까?
B: 아니요, 얼마나 빠른지 몰라요.

④ A: 한국에 외국인이 몇 명쯤 사는지 압니까?
B: 아니요, 몇 명쯤 사는지 몰라요.

⑤ A: 현재 한국의 대통령이 누구인지 압니까?
B: 네, 누구인지 알아요.

Grammar Focus

(으)로 해서 is used to indicate that something goes via a certain spot or goes through the spot. It is attached to a noun, and if the noun ends in a consonant 으로 해서 is used, while 로 해서 is used if it ends in the consonant ㄹ or a vowel.

Noun	(으)로 해서	Noun	(으)로 해서
제주도	제주도로 해서	일본	일본으로 해서
서울	서울로 해서	명동	명동으로 해서

ex A: 명동까지 어떻게 가야 합니까?
B: 종로로 해서 가세요.

ex A: 화장실이 어디에 있어요?
B: 사무실 왼쪽 옆으로 해서 가면 화장실이 있어요.

ex A: 밤이라서 길이 많이 어두워요.
B: 네. 어두우니까 큰길로 해서 갑시다.

Focus Plus

- (으)로 can be used to indicate the direction of a certain spot or a destination, or to indicate the means or method of a certain behavior. (See 『이화 한국어 1-1』 Chapter 4, p.73, and 『이화 한국어 1-1』 Chapter 11, p.66)

ex A: 실례합니다. 백화점이 어디에 있습니까?
B: 오른쪽으로 가세요. 지하철역 옆에 있습니다.

ex A: 학교에 어떻게 가요?
B: 저는 보통 지하철로 가요.

Answers

① A: 7011번 버스는 월드컵경기장까지 어디로 해서 갑니까?
B: 이대역으로 해서 갑니다.

② A: 143번 버스는 압구정동까지 어디로 해서 갑니까?
B: 이태원으로 해서 갑니다.

③ A: 603번 버스는 신촌역까지 어디로 해서 갑니까?
B: 서울역으로 해서 갑니다.

④ A: 507번 버스는 명동까지 어디로 해서 갑니까?
B: 숭례문으로 해서 갑니다.

⑤ A: 8000번 버스는 국립민속박물관까지 어디로 해서 갑니까?
B: 경복궁으로 해서 갑니다.

Grammar Focus

–자마자 is used to indicate that an occasion or situation occurs and is followed right away by another occasion or situation. So the time interval between the previous situation and the following situation is very short. It is attached to a verb and is used whether the verb stem ends in a consonant or a vowel. Generally, negative expressions are not used in the previous clause connected with –자마자.

Basic form	–자마자	Basic form	–자마자
가다	가자마자	듣다	듣자마자
쓰다	쓰자마자	살다	살자마자
입다	입자마자	돕다	돕자마자
읽다	읽자마자	붓다	붓자마자

ex A: 오늘 수업 끝나고 같이 점심을 먹을까요?
B: 미안해요. 오늘 수업이 끝나자마자 바로 병원에 가야 해요.

ex A: 커피를 마시러 갈 건데 같이 갈래요?
B: 아니요. 전 괜찮아요. 아침을 먹자마자 이미 한 잔 마셨거든요.

ex A: 퇴근 시간에 전화했었는데 통화가 안 돼서 걱정했어요.
B: 퇴근하고 택시를 타자마자 잠이 들어서 전화를 못 받았어요.

ex A: 유키 씨, 괜찮아요? 교통사고 소식을 듣자마자 병원으로 바로 달려왔어요.
B: 괜찮아요. 큰 사고가 아니었어요. 신경 써 줘서 고마워요.

ex A: 집에 안 오자마자 친구를 만났어요. (×)
B: 한국어를 모르자마자 선생님께 질문하세요. (×)

Focus Plus

- –는 대로 is used to indicate 'as soon as' an action occurs. A coincidental situation can be used after –자마자, but not after –는 대로. The past tense can be used in a sentence that is connected with –자마자, but not in a sentence with –는 대로. (See 「이화 한국어 2–2」 Chapter 10. p.56)

  ex 버스를 타자마자 배가 아팠어요. (○)
  버스를 타는 대로 배가 아팠어요. (×)

Answers

① 나타샤 씨는 집에 들어오자마자 손을 씻습니다.
② 마이클 씨는 졸업하자마자 취직했습니다.
③ 왕카이 씨는 침대에 눕자마자 잠이 들었습니다.

Vocabulary & Expression

교통비도 줄일 수 있고

교통비도 줄일 수 있고 means ***that (you) can also save on travel expenses***. 줄이다 means to reduce the number or amount of something. It is used in expressions such as 교통비를 줄이다, 여행 경비를 줄이다, 식사량을 줄이다, and 몸무게를 줄이다.

ex A: 요즘 기름값이 너무 비싸서 걱정이에요.
B: 맞아요. 그래서 자동차를 직접 운전하는 것보다 대중교통을 이용하면 교통비를 줄일 수 있어요.

ex A: 어떻게 하면 여행 경비를 줄일 수 있을까요?
B: 주말보다 평일에 출발하는 비행기 표를 예매하면 교통비를 줄일 수 있을 거예요.

ex A: 어떻게 살을 뺐어요?
B: 식사량을 줄이고 운동을 열심히 했어요.

당장

당장 means ***right away***.

ex A: 주말에는 기차를 타는 사람들이 많으니까 기차표를 빨리 예약합시다.
B: 그래요? 당장 기차표를 예약할게요.

ex A: 날씨가 참 좋네요. 한강으로 소풍 가고 싶어요.
B: 그래요? 그럼 오늘 당장 가요.

ex A: 머리가 너무 아파서 못 일어나겠어요.
B: 정말요? 지금 당장 병원에 가는 게 좋겠어요.

교통편과 숙소

교통편과 숙소 means ***transportation and accommodation***. 교통편 is a means of transportation used to get from one place to another. 숙소 means accommodation, a place where one stays temporarily away from home. They are used in expressions such as 교통편을 알아보다, 숙소를 알아보다, and 숙소를 잡다.

ex A: 왕카이 씨, 지금 뭐 하고 있어요?
B: 친구와 제주도를 여행하려고 지금 인터넷에서 교통편과 숙소를 알아보는 중이에요.

ex A: 부산에 갈 때 어떤 교통편을 이용할 거예요?
B: 기차를 이용하려고 해요.

ex A: 여행지에서 묵을 숙소는 정하셨어요?
B: 아니요. 요즘은 휴가철이라 숙소를 잡기가 어렵네요.

Functional Expression

- **Asking if there is another way**

When asking if there is another way, expressions such as 다른 방법은 없어요?, 다른 좋은 방법은 없을까요?, 다른 방법에는 뭐가 있을까요?, 다른 방법에는 어떤 게 있어요? can be used.

ex A: 제주도까지 배를 타고 가는 게 가장 싸지만 시간이 너무 많이 걸려요.
B: 그럼 다른 방법은 없어요? /
그래요? 다른 좋은 방법은 없을까요? /
그래요? 다른 방법에는 뭐가 있을까요? /
그렇군요. 그럼 다른 방법에는 어떤 게 있어요?

Script

Zhang Souyi	Hyeonmi, I'd like to go to Jeju Island as soon as this semester ends, but I am not so sure how to get there.
Park Hyeonmi	There are many ways to get to Jeju Island. But the easiest way is to take a plane. It only takes about an hour by plane.
Zhang Souyi	I see. But isn't it a little expensive? Isn't there a cheaper way to get there?
Park Hyeonmi	The cheapest way to Jeju Island is to take the subway to Incheon and then take a boat. But it takes too long.
Zhang Souyi	Really? Aren't there any decent alternatives?
Park Hyeonmi	Going via Gwangju is also a good option. You take the express bus to Gwangju and take a plane from there. If you take the bus, you can cut transportation costs and enjoy the great scenery as well.
Zhang Souyi	That sounds like a good way to go.
Park Hyeonmi	But a lot of people travel during the vacation season, so you should hurry and make reservations in advance.
Zhang Souyi	Really? Then I'll go and make reservations for the transportation and accommodation right away.

Answers

(1) ③
The ticket for an express bus to Gwangju and then a plane to Jeju Island is number ③.

(2) ③
If you take the plane to Jeju Island you can reduce time but not the expense.

(3) ① 아니요 ② 아니요 ③ 아니요
Zhang Souyi is going to go to Jeju Island as soon as the semester ends. As many people travel in the vacation season, a ticket has to be reserved in advance. But it is uncertain whether the seats are already sold out. As she has not yet made reservations for transportation and accommodation, she is going to do that right away.

택배 기사에게 길 알려 주기

p.96

Vocabulary & Expression

우회전을 하세요

우회전을 하세요 means ***make a right turn***. When giving directions, expressions such as 우회전하다, 좌회전하다, 직진하다 can be used. 우회전하다 means to turn to the right, 좌회전하다 means to turn to the left, and 직진하다 means to go straight.

ex A: 영화관에 가려면 어떻게 가야 돼요?
B: 학교 정문에서 우회전한 다음에 직진하세요. 그럼 오른쪽에 영화관이 보일 거예요.

Functional Expression

- **Giving directions to one's house**

When giving directions to your house, you can use expressions such as N이/가 보일 겁니다, N이/가 나올 거예요, N이/가 있어요, N이/가 있을 거예요 etc.

ex A: 이대역 사거리에서 이화 아파트까지 어떻게 가야 합니까?
B: 거기에서 우회전을 하면 왼쪽에 이화 아파트가 보일 겁니다. /
거기에서 오른쪽으로 돌면 왼쪽에 이화 아파트가 나올 거예요. /
거기에서 우회전을 하세요. 그러면 왼쪽에 이화 아파트가 있어요. /
거기에서 오른쪽으로 돌자마자 왼쪽에 이화 아파트가 있을 거예요.

Dialogue

Natasha	Hello?
Deliveryman	This is Ewha Delivery. Is this Natasha's residence?
Natasha	Yes, it is.
Deliveryman	I'm on my way to your house with the goods you ordered. I'm in Myeong-dong right now. Can you tell me how I can get to your house from here?
Natasha	From there you can reach our house by way of City Hall or Seoul Station.
Deliveryman	Which way is faster?
Natasha	Passing City Hall is the fastest way, and there's not a lot of traffic there.
Deliveryman	I see. Then can you give me directions from City Hall?
Natasha	From City Hall, keep going straight to Ahyeon-dong and you'll see Subway Line No. 2.
Deliveryman	Okay. How do I proceed from there?
Natasha	Make a right turn at the Ewha Station intersection. If you go about 80m ahead, there is a coffee shop on the left. As soon as you pass the coffee shop, make a left and you'll see Ewha Apartment.
Deliveryman	Alright, thanks. I'll be there right away.

Grammar Focus

–았/었다가 is used to indicate a change in action or situation after a certain action or situation is completed. It is attached to a verb and is used when the situations in the preceding and following clauses are conflicting or opposite. –았다가 is used when the last vowel in the adjective stem is ㅏ or ㅗ. For all other vowel endings of the adjective or verb stem –었다가 is used.

Basic form	–았/었다가	Basic form	–았/었다가	Basic form	–았/었다가
가다	갔다가	듣다	들었다가	돕다	도왔다가
입다	입었다가	살다	살았다가	짓다	지었다가

ex A: 티엔 씨, 버스를 타고 왔어요?
B: 아니요. 택시를 탔다가 차가 너무 밀려서 지하철로 갈아탔어요.

ex A: 마이클 씨 오늘 모자를 쓰고 오지 않았어요?
B: 네. 그런데 더워서 모자를 썼다가 벗었어요.

ex A: 교실이 좀 추운 것 같아요.
B: 아, 제가 좀 전에 창문을 열었다가 닫았거든요.

Focus Plus

- –았/었다가 and –다가 are similar in that they indicate a change in action. However, –다가 is used to indicate a change in situation in the middle of a situation or when it is interrupted, while –았/었다가 is used when a situation is completed and changes to a different situation. (See 『이화 한국어 2–2』 Chapter 10, p.64)

  ex 집에 가다가 서점에 들렀어요. (= 집에 가는 길에 서점에 들렀어요)
  집에 갔다가 서점에 갔어요. (= 집에 갔어요. 그리고 다시 서점에 갔어요)

- –았/었다가 is used when the action in the previous clause becomes the reason or grounds for what happens in the following clause.

  ex A: 둘이 어떻게 같이 와요?
  B: 학교 앞 서점에 들렀다가 거기에서 우연히 만났어요. 그래서 같이 왔어요.

Answers

① 창문을 열었다가 비가 와서 닫았어요.
② 텔레비전을 켰다가 재미있는 프로그램을 하지 않아서 껐어요.
③ 높은 구두를 신었다가 불편해서 벗었어요.
④ 빨간색 넥타이를 맸다가 안 어울려서 풀었어요.
⑤ 인터넷으로 옷을 주문했다가 마음이 바뀌어서 취소했어요.

Grammar Focus

-(으)ㄹ 테니까 is used to express the speaker's strong speculation regarding the following clause. It is usually followed by a suggestion or a request to the listener in the following clause. It is attached to an adjective or a verb, and if the stem of the adjective or verb ends in a consonant -을 테니까 is used, while -ㄹ 테니까 is used if it ends in the consonant ㄹ or a vowel. The subject can only be second or third person, not the speaker.

Basic form	-(으)ㄹ 테니까	-았/었을 테니까	Basic form	-(으)ㄹ 테니까	-았/었을 테니까
싸다	쌀 테니까	쌌을 테니까	오다	올 테니까	왔을 테니까
크다	클 테니까	컸을 테니까	입다	입을 테니까	입었을 테니까
작다	작을 테니까	작았을 테니까	듣다	들을 테니까	들었을 테니까
많다	많을 테니까	많았을 테니까	팔다	팔 테니까	팔았을 테니까
멀다	멀 테니까	멀었을 테니까	돕다	도울 테니까	도왔을 테니까
덥다	더울 테니까	더웠을 테니까	짓다	지을 테니까	지었을 테니까

ex A: 어디에서 장을 볼까요?
B: 백화점은 비쌀 테니까 시장에 가서 장을 봅시다.

ex A: 오후에 손님이 오실 테니까 청소 좀 합시다.
B: 네, 알겠습니다.

ex A: 비가 너무 많이 오는데 비행기가 제시간에 출발할 수 있을까요?
B: 네, 비행기는 제시간에 출발할 테니까 걱정하지 마세요.

ex A: 나타샤 씨, 어디에 가요?
B: (나는) 감기에 걸릴 것 같아서 약을 사러 약국에 가는 중이에요. (○)
(나는) 감기에 걸릴 테니까 약을 사러 약국에 가는 중이에요. (×)

Answers

① A: 이번 시험이 어려울까요?
B: 네. 시험이 어려울 테니까 준비를 철저히 하세요.

② A: 오후에 비가 올까요?
B: 네. 비가 올 테니까 우산을 가지고 가세요.

③ A: 주말에 백화점이 붐빌까요?
B: 네. 주말에는 백화점이 붐빌 테니까 금요일에 장을 보세요.

④ A: 새로 시작한 사업이 잘 될까요?
B: 네. 사업이 잘 될 테니까 걱정하지 마세요.

⑤ A: 다음에 장학금을 받을 수 있을까요?
B: 네. 다음에는 장학금을 받을 수 있을 테니까 지금부터 열심히 준비하세요.

Vocabulary & Expression

피하시는 것이 좋겠습니다

피하시는 것이 좋겠습니다 means ***it would be better if (you) could avoid (it).*** It indicates that it is better to avoid something and go another way. 피하다 means to avoid something that you don't want to happen to you and to prevent trouble.

ex A: 올림픽대로 방향은 길이 많이 막히니까 피하시는 것이 좋겠습니다.
B: 네, 알겠습니다.

ex A: 주말인데 빨리 도착했군요.
B: 우리가 탄 차는 복잡한 도로를 피해서 차가 없는 도로로 왔거든요.

Functional Expression

- **Giving directions to the final destination**

When telling the driver which road to take to your destination, you can use expressions such as 'N쪽 N을/를 타세요, N 방향 N(으)로 가세요, N 방향 N(으)로 가면 돼요 etc.

ex A: 여기에서 여의도에 가려고 하는데 어떻게 가야 돼요?
B: 여기에서 김포공항 쪽 올림픽대로를 타세요. /
여기에서 김포공항 방향 올림픽대로로 가세요. /
여기에서 김포공항 방향 올림픽대로로 가면 돼요.

Script

Good morning. This is your morning traffic report. Right now, the roads are quite bad because of the fog. Traffic on the Olympic Expressway in the Gimpo direction is especially heavy. If you take the Olympic Expressway, it will take longer than usual so try to avoid it. Also there is a run-down car at the entrance to the Gyeongbu Expressway from Seoul. So a lot of cars that have entered the Gyeongbu Expressway are now turning to take another road. Seocho Interchange on the Gyeongbu Expressway is the worst of all right now, so it would be a good idea to take the Yangjae Interchange instead.

This afternoon an event is scheduled to be held in front of Seoul City Hall and the roads in the area will be closed from this afternoon. Keep this in mind if you're heading toward City Hall today.

Please drive safely. This has been Lee Jinhee from Traffic Broadcasting System.

Answers

(1) ② Traffic on the Olympic Expressway is very heavy because of fog.

(2) 서초 인터체인지
The reporter said Seocho Interchange was the most heavily congested place.

(3) ① 아니요　② 네　③ 아니요
As the Olympic Expressway is especially jammed, taking this road will be slow. Because an event will be held in front of Seoul Plaza this afternoon, the roads around City Hall will be closed from the afternoon. They will not be closed all day.

Vocabulary & Expression

배터리

배터리 means ***battery***. It is a device that supplies the electricity needed to operate cars, mobile phones, watches and other things. It is used in expressions such as 배터리가 없다 and 배터리를 충전하다.

ex A: 왕카이 씨, 왜 이렇게 늦었어요? 전화도 안 받고요.
B: 미안해요. 배터리가 없어서 전화를 받을 수 없었어요.
A: 다음부터는 집에서 나오기 전에 배터리를 충전하세요.
B: 네, 알겠어요. 늦어서 미안해요.

ex A: 시계가 멈추었어요.
B: 배터리가 없는 것 같아요. 배터리를 새 것으로 바꾸세요.

훨씬

훨씬 means ***much more***. It indicates that something is very different when compared with something else. It is used in front of an adjective.

ex A: 지하철을 타지 않고 버스를 타고 왔어요?
B: 보통은 버스가 훨씬 빨라서 탔는데 오늘은 길이 너무 막혔어요.

ex A: 부산까지 어떻게 가는 게 좋아요?
B: KTX를 타고 가세요. KTX가 다른 기차보다 훨씬 빠르거든요.

ex A: 새로 이사한 집은 어때요?
B: 교통도 편리하고 전에 살던 집보다 훨씬 커서 좋아요.

꼼짝도 안 했어요

꼼짝도 안 했어요 means ***(it) would not budge***. It indicates that something or someone did not move at all. When an object or a person does not move at all, you can use 꼼짝도 안 하다. Usually, a negative expression such as 안 하다 or 못 하다 comes after 꼼짝.

ex A: 왜 이렇게 늦었어요? 차가 많이 막혔어요?
B: 네, 신촌까지 빨리 왔는데 신촌부터 차가 밀려서 차가 꼼짝도 안 했어요.

ex A: 책장을 옮겨야 하는데 책장이 꼼짝도 안 해요. 좀 도와주세요.
B: 네, 알겠어요.

ex A: 주말에 뭐 했어요?
B: 너무 피곤해서 꼼짝도 안 하고 집에서 쉬었어요.

ex A: 다리를 많이 다쳤다고 들었어요.
B: 네. 그래서 며칠 동안 꼼짝 못하고 누워만 있었어요.

Functional Expression

- **Saying one was late because of traffic congestion**

When you explain that you are late because of a traffic jam, you can say 차가 밀려서 늦었어요, 길이 막혀서 일찍 올 수 없었어요, 길이 막혀서 차가 꼼짝도 안 했어요, 차가 밀려서 시내가 주차장처럼 되었어요, 차가 움직이지 않고 계속 길에 서 있었어요, 도로가 정체돼서 시간이 많이 걸렸어요 etc.

ex A: 왜 이렇게 늦었어요? 무슨 일이 있었어요?
B: 길이 너무 막혀서 늦었어요. /
차가 밀려서 일찍 올 수 없었어요. /
길이 막혀서 차가 꼼짝도 안 했어요. /
차가 밀려서 시내가 주차장처럼 되었어요. /
차가 움직이지 않고 계속 길에 서 있었어요. /
도로가 정체돼서 오는 데 시간이 많이 걸렸어요.

- **Saying a situation was unavoidable**

When you want to explain that something could not be avoided, you can say 어쩔 수 없었군요, 어떻게 할 수 없었네요, 다른 방법이 없었겠네요, 어쩔 수 없는 상황이었군요 etc. 어쩔 수 없다, indicating that there is nothing you can do.

ex A: 지하철이 고장 나서 늦었어요. 정말 미안해요.
B: 그래요? 장소이 씨도 어쩔 수 없었군요. /
아니에요. 장소이 씨도 어떻게 할 수 없었네요. /
괜찮아요. 장소이 씨도 다른 방법이 없었겠네요. /
괜찮아요. 장소이 씨도 어쩔 수 없는 상황이었군요.

Dialogue

Zhang Souyi	Tien, you must have been waiting for a long time.
Tien	What happened?
Zhang Souyi	The traffic was awful. I'm sorry I'm so late.
Tien	You didn't answer your phone and since you didn't show up even after an hour, I was really worried.
Zhang Souyi	I was going to call you but my battery ran out.
Tien	But did you take the bus here, not the subway?
Zhang Souyi	I took the bus because it's usually much faster, but the traffic was so heavy today. So I took the bus and then switched to the subway.
Tien	Why were the roads so bad today?
Zhang Souyi	There was an event in front of City Hall and the cars were not budging.
Tien	I see. You must be worn out by now. Let's go eat.
Zhang Souyi	I'm really sorry for being so late today.
Tien	It's okay. You couldn't do anything about it.

Vocabulary & Expression

대중교통을 이용합니다

대중교통을 이용합니다 means ***(I) use public transportation***. 이용하다 is to make use of something as needed. 사용하다 is similar to 이용하다. However, 사용하다 is to use an object for a certain purpose or according to its function, as in 휴대 전화를 사용하다, 컴퓨터를 사용하다 etc. When you talk about public transportation, 이용하다 is generally used instead of 사용하다.

ex A: 출근할 때 대중교통을 이용합니까?
B: 네. 차가 막히는 출퇴근 시간에는 대중교통을 이용합니다.

ex 한국에서는 어떤 대중교통을 많이 이용합니까? (○)
한국에서는 어떤 대중교통을 많이 사용합니까? (×)

ex 수업 시간에 휴대 전화를 사용하지 마세요.(○)
수업 시간에 휴대 전화를 이용하지 마세요.(×)

갈아타는 경우

갈아타는 경우 means ***in case (you) transfer***. It indicates the transfer from one means of transportation to another. -는 경우 is used to talk about a certain condition or circumstance.

ex A: 교통카드를 사용하면 뭐가 좋아요?
B: 대중교통으로 갈아타는 경우 교통비가 할인되어서 좋아요.

ex A: 같이 여행 갈 사람이 없어서 혼자 가는 경우 저에게 연락 주세요.
지금 같이 여행 갈 사람을 찾고 있거든요.
B: 네, 알겠어요.

못 잊을 경험이 될 겁니다

못 잊을 경험이 될 겁니다 means ***it will be an unforgettable experience***. This expression indicates that something will be an experience one will never forget. When you talk about an experience that is wonderful or very meaningful, you can use 못 잊을 경험.

ex A: 다른 나라에 여행을 가면 그 나라의 대중교통을 꼭 이용해 보세요.
못 잊을 경험이 될 겁니다.
B: 그렇군요. 꼭 이용해 볼게요.

ex A: 제주도 여행 어땠어요?
B: 매우 좋았어요. 이치로 씨도 꼭 한번 가 보세요. 못 잊을 경험이 될 거예요.

Pronunciation

ㄴ addition

When there is a final consonant in the word in front and the word following starts with 이, 야, 여, 요, 유, 얘, or 예, [ㄴ] should be added in between for proper pronunciation. This phenomenon is called ㄴ addition.

ex 이용 요금[이용뇨금], 급한 일[그판닐], 배낭 여행[배낭녀행], 못 잊을[몬니즐]

Text

There are various kinds of public transportation systems in each country. Do you know what kinds of transportation are often used in South Korea and Bangladesh?

The most popular means of transportation in Korea are the subway, buses, and taxis. Buses and the subway are used by many people because they are fast. Public transportation is especially convenient if you have to pass through the downtown area to go somewhere else. Since buses use the bus-only lanes, they are not caught in traffic and the subway is good because it saves you time. Also, when you transfer to another form of public transportation, you can get a discount on the fare.

There are buses, taxis, and rickshaws for public transportation in Bangladesh. In particular, rickshaws are used by a lot by people. Tourists also use rickshaws when they go to Bangladesh on backpacking trips or on business trips. The rickshaw is a special form of transportation that is made by converting a bicycle. You can use a rickshaw on a rainy day since there is a roof installed over the seat.

People like to use rickshaws because they are cheap. Also, a rickshaw can easily pass through small alleyways difficult for cars to navigate, so it can be used for urgent matters or when you are late for an appointment.

As can be seen, different countries have different types of public transportation. If you travel to another country, as soon as you get there you can easily see the country's unique transportation system, so give it a try. It will be an unforgettable experience.

Answers

(1) 한국과 방글라데시의 대중교통

(2) ①

People use buses or the subway a lot because they are fast.

(3) ① 아니요　② 아니요　③ 네

A rickshaw can be used on a rainy day since there is a roof installed over the seat. They can easily pass through small alleyways. Also, since the fare (transportation fee) is cheap, they are used by many people.

(4) 지하철: ① 빠릅니다.　② 시간을 절약할 수 있습니다.

릭샤 : ① 비가 오는 날에도 탈 수 있습니다.　② 이용 요금이 쌉니다.　③ 좁은 골목길도 쉽게 다닐 수 있습니다.

Vocabulary Check

▶ **Tick off the words and expressions that you know.**

교통	Transportation
☐ 교통사고가 나다	to get into a car accident
☐ 교통이 편하다	to have good transportation
☐ 교통편을 알아보다	to find out about transportation
☐ 교통편을 예약하다	to book transportation
☐ 교통편이 나쁘다	to have bad transportation
☐ 길을 막다	to block traffic
☐ 길이 막히다	to be congested (traffic, roads)
☐ 다른 길로 돌아가다	to take a detour
☐ 대중교통을 이용하다	to use public transportation
☐ 버스가 고장 나다	to have a bus break down
☐ 버스를 놓치다	to miss a bus
☐ 빠른 길로 가다	to go the fast way
☐ 신호가 바뀌다	to change (the traffic light)
☐ 신호를 어기다	to violate a traffic signal
☐ 우등 고속버스를 타다	to take a premium express bus
☐ 음주 운전하다	to drink and drive
☐ 정체되다	to be congested (traffic, roads, etc)
☐ 차가 밀리다	to have traffic congestion
☐ 차가 움직이지 않다	to have traffic that is not moving/ to have the cars remain still
☐ 택시를 잡다	to take a taxi

도로	Roads
☐ 경부고속도로	Gyeongbu Expressway
☐ 골목길	alley
☐ 교차로	crossroad, intersection
☐ 로터리	rotary
☐ 버스 전용차로	exclusive bus lane
☐ 사거리	crossroad
☐ 삼거리	three-way junction
☐ 올림픽대로	Olympic Highway
☐ 인터체인지	interchange

길 안내	Giving Directions
☐ 골목길로 가다	to go via the alleys
☐ 똑바로 가다	to go straight
☐ 목적지에 도착하다	to arrive at one's destination
☐ 빠른 길을 알려주다	to inform someone of a shortcut
☐ 오른쪽으로 가다	to go right
☐ 왼쪽으로 가다	to go left
☐ 우회전하다	to turn right
☐ 좌회전하다	to turn left
☐ 지하철 노선도를 보다	to look at the subway map
☐ 직진하다	to go straight
☐ 쭉 가다	to go straight ahead

숙소	Accommodation
☐ 묵을 곳을 찾다	to look for somewhere to lodge
☐ 숙박비가 할인되다	to have accommodation discounted
☐ 숙박비를 알아보다	to look for accommodation
☐ 숙소를 잡다	to book accommodation
☐ 숙소를 정하다	to decide where to stay
☐ 싼 곳에 묵다	to stay somewhere cheap
☐ 호텔을 알아보다	to look for a hotel

PART1 준비합시다 01 • –아/어야겠–

p.110

Grammar Focus

–아/어야겠– is used to express a strong will for an action that ought to take place or should not fail to take place. It is usually used colloquially while –아/어야 하겠– is used in a written context. It is attached to a verb.

Basic form	–아/어야겠다	Basic form	–아/어야겠다
가다	가야겠다	만들다	만들어야겠다
고르다	골라야겠다	돕다	도와야겠다
찾다	찾아야겠다	걷다	걸어야겠다
먹지 말다	먹지 말아야겠다	붓다	부어야겠다

ex A: 오늘 슈퍼에 가죠? 뭘 살 거예요?
B: 휴지가 떨어졌어요. 휴지를 좀 사야겠어요.

ex A: 차 열쇠 주세요. 제가 운전할게요.
B: 어! 열쇠가 없어요. 아까 배낭에 넣은 것 같은데 다시 찾아봐야겠어요.

ex A: 어디 불편해요? 머리가 아파요?
B: 네. 두통약을 먹어야겠어요.

ex A: 교실이 덥지요? 창문을 좀 열까요?
B: 네, 좀 열어야겠어요. 너무 더워요.

ex A: 티엔 씨, 점심 잘 먹었어요. 그런데 너무 많이 먹은 거 같아요.
B: 저도요. 소화가 되게 좀 걸어야겠어요. 같이 걸을래요?

ex A: 수잔 씨, 라면에 물이 너무 적어요.
B: 그래요? 그럼 물을 좀 더 부어야겠네요.

ex A: 요즘 건강이 안 좋은 것 같아요. 병원에 다녀왔어요?
B: 네. 이제 술을 마시지 말아야겠어요. 의사 선생님도 그렇게 말씀하셨어요.

Answers

① A: 장소이 씨, 요즘도 두통이 심해요?
B: 네. 너무 아파서 병원에서 진찰을 받아야겠어요.

② A: 왕카이 씨, 컴퓨터가 또 고장 났어요?
B: 네. 고장이 자주 나서 새 걸로 바꿔야겠어요.

③ A: 나타샤 씨, 티엔 씨가 오늘도 결석했어요?
B: 네. 걱정이 돼서 티엔 씨에게 전화해 봐야겠어요.

④ A: 미셸 씨, 오늘 아침을 안 먹었어요?
B: 네. 배가 너무 고파서 간단한 걸 먹어야겠어요.

⑤ A: 얀 씨, 같은 방 친구가 매일 밤늦게까지 전화해요?
B: 네. 잠을 잘 수 없어서 그 친구에게 이야기해야겠어요.

02 • 아무도, 아무것도, 아무 데도

p.111

Grammar Focus

아무도, 아무것도 and 아무 데도 refer to a nonspecific person, object and place. 아무도 means 어느 누구도, 아무것도 means 어느 것도, and 아무 데도 means 어느 곳에도. In the form of 아무+N, expressions such as 아무 말도, 아무 소용도, 아무 방에도 and 아무 직원에게도 are used. They are followed by a negative expression.

누구?	아무도	어디에?	아무 데도
무엇?	아무것도	어디에서?	아무 데서도
언제?	아무 때도	누구에게/한테?	아무에게도/한테도
무슨 말?	아무 말도	누구에게서/한테서?	아무에게서도/한테서도

ex A: 미셸 씨, 생일 선물 많이 받았어요?
B: 아니요. 우리 반 친구들은 아무도 제 생일이 언제인지 몰라요.

ex A: 어제 남대문 시장에 가서 뭐 샀어요?
B: 아무것도 안 샀어요. 구경만 했어요.

ex A: 수잔 씨, 지갑 찾았어요?
B: 아니요. 다 찾아봤는데 아무 데도 없어요.

ex A: 새로 나온 수박 아이스크림 먹어 봤어요?
B: 아니요. 나오자마자 다 팔려서 아무 데서도 살 수가 없어요.

ex A: 이 말은 다른 사람들에게 절대로 하지 말아 주세요.
B: 걱정 마세요. 아무한테도 이야기 안 할게요.

ex A: 우리 딸이 공부는 안 하고 가수가 되려고 연습실에 다녀요. 제가 말을 했지만 듣지 않아요.
B: 따님이 노래 잘하잖아요. 가수도 좋아요. 그냥 아무 말도 말고 좀 하고 싶은 일을 하게 해 보세요.

Answers

① A: 집들이 선물로 가루비누나 휴지를 준비했어요?
B: 아니요. 시간이 없어서 아무것도 준비 못 했어요.

② A: 한국에서 부산이나 제주도에 여행 가 봤어요?
B: 아니요. 일이 너무 많아서 아무 데도 못 가 봤어요.

③ A: 얀 씨 생일을 다른 사람이 알고 있어요?
B: 아니요. 얀 씨가 말하지 않아서 아무도 몰랐어요.

④ A: 담배를 교실이나 휴게실에서 피울 수 있어요?
B: 아니요. 학교는 금연 구역이라서 아무 데에서도 담배를 피울 수 없어요.

⑤ A: 약속 시간이 바뀐 걸 마이클 씨나 티엔 씨에게서 연락받았어요?
B: 아니요. 오늘 휴대 전화를 안 가져와서 아무에게도 전화를 못 받았어요.

 p.112

Grammar Focus

-기(가) 쉽다 is used when a certain matter or situation is likely to or tends to happen. -기(가) is followed by 어렵다, 힘들다, 좋다, 싫다, 즐겁다, 편하다, 불편하다 etc.

Basic form	-기(가) 쉽다/어렵다	-기(가) 편하다/불편하다
갈아타다	갈아타기(가) 쉽다/어렵다	갈아타기(가) 편하다/불편하다
읽다	읽기(가) 쉽다/어렵다	읽기(가) 편하다/불편하다
만들다	만들기(가) 쉽다/어렵다	만들기(가) 편하다/불편하다

ex A: 서울에서 지하철을 갈아타기가 어때요?
B: 어렵지 않아요. 지도가 있으면 쉽게 갈아탈 수 있어요.

ex A: 이 길은 높은 구두를 신고 걷기 힘들어요.
B: 맞아요. 길에 돌이 많아서 힘드네요.

ex A: 이 책은 아이들이 읽기 쉬워요?
B: 네, 어렵지도 않고 그림도 많아서 쉬워요.

ex A: 이 국자 어디에서 샀어요? 참 젓기 편하게 만들었네요.
B: 그래요? 우리 집 앞 슈퍼마켓에서 샀어요.

Focus Plus

- -기 and -(으)ㅁ are both endings attached to the verb stems, adjective stems, 이다, and 아니다 to make them act as nouns that serve as the subject or object in a sentence. However, -(으)ㅁ is more frequently used than -기 to refer to a fact that is already known or has taken place. -기 is accompanied by 쉽다, 어렵다, 힘들다 or 좋아하다, 싫어하다, 바라다, 시작하다, 약속하다. On the other hand, -(으)ㅁ is used with 잊어버리다, 알다, 보고하다, 알리다, etc.

ex 우리를 가장 사랑하는 사람이 부모님임을 잊어버리지 마. (○)
우리를 가장 사랑하는 사람이 부모님이기를 잊어버리지 마. (×)
민호 씨가 시험에 합격했음을 알렸다. (○)
민호 씨가 시험에 합격하기를 알렸다. (×)

Answers

① A: 서울에서 길 찾기가 어때요?
B: 작은 골목이 많아서 찾기가 어려워요.

② A: 서울에서 취직하기가 어때요?
B: 한국어를 잘 못해서 취직하기가 어려워요.

③ A: 서울에서 물건 사기가 어때요?
B: 싸고 좋은 가게가 많아서 사기가 편해요.

④ A: 서울에서 병원 이용하기가 어때요?
B: 외국인 통역 서비스가 있어서 이용하기가 편해요.

⑤ A: 서울에서 시내에 주차하기가 어때요?
B: 주차장이 많지 않아서 주차하기가 불편해요.

PART1 들어 봅시다 부동산 소개소에서 집 구하는 대화 듣기

p.113

Vocabulary & Expression

오피스텔

오피스텔 means ***an officetel***. It is an accommodation equipped with simple living facilities which functions as both an office and residence. It is a compound word of 'office' and 'hotel' and is similar to a studio apartment or efficiency apartment.

ex A: 요코 씨, 어디에 살아요? 사무실이 집에서 가까워요?
B: 전 회사 앞에 있는 오피스텔에 살아요. 그래서 일하기가 정말 편해요.

ex A: 마이클 씨, 요즘 학생들이 학교 근처 오피스텔에 많이 살지요?
B: 네. 크지 않지만 아파트처럼 방에 부엌도 있고 화장실도 있어서 학생들이 많이 찾아요.

가격이 높습니다

가격이 높습니다 means ***the price is high***. On the contrary, you can say 가격이 낮다, 가격이 저렴하다 when the price is low.

ex A: 손님, 이 집은 다른 집에 비해 가격이 높지만 교통이 편해서 좋을 겁니다.
B: 네. 마음에는 들어요. 그런데 좀 생각해 보고 다시 올게요.

ex A: 마이클 씨, 이 침대가 마음에 드는데 다른 것보다 비싼 거 같아요, 싼 거 같아요?
B: 가격이 좀 높은 거 같아요.

Functional Expression

- **Asking the size of the house someone is looking for**

  When a real estate agent asks his/her client about the size of the house they are looking for, expressions such as 집이 얼마나 큰 걸 찾으세요?, 방 몇 개짜리 집을 구하시나요?, 어느 정도 크기를 찾으십니까? or 집 크기가 어느 정도이면 됩니까? are used.

  ex A: 집이 얼마나 큰 걸 찾으세요? /
  방 몇 개짜리 집을 구하시나요? /
  어느 정도 크기를 찾으십니까? /
  집 크기가 어느 정도이면 됩니까?
  B: 방 2개에 화장실 하나, 부엌 정도면 됩니다.

- **Talking about the price of monthly rent and *Jeonse***

  Prices sometimes change according to the conditions of purchase. This also applies when buying a house. In Korea, there are two ways to rent a house: Jeonse and monthly rent. *Jeonse* is a legal agreement by which the tenant pays the owner of the house a lump sum to live in the house for 1-2 years and receives the money back from the owner when he/she moves out. Monthly rent is paying rent on a house once every month. *Jeonse* and monthly rent can be partially combined. Therefore, in order to talk about the price for renting a house according to various conditions, expressions such as 전세 ○천만 원, 월세 ○만 원이에요, 전세로 ○원이고, 월세로 하면 ○입니다 or 전세로 하면 ○천만 원이고 월세로 하면 ○천만 원에 ○만 원이에요 are used.

ex A: 가격이 어떻게 돼요?

B: 전세 5천만 원, 월세 50만 원이에요. /
전세로 하면 5천이고 월세로 하면 50입니다. /
전세 5천만 원, 월세로 하면 2천만 원에 50만 원입니다.

Script

Agent	Come in. What are you looking for?
Michelle	I'm looking for an officetel.
Agent	Please have a seat. What size are you looking for?
Michelle	I'm going to live with a friend, so two bedrooms will do.
Agent	Really? I have a good one for you. It has two bedrooms, a kitchen, and bathroom. It's near the school and there is a discount store nearby, so it will be convenient to live in.
Michelle	That sounds good. How much is it?
Agent	It is 50 million won for *jeonse*, or 500,000 won in monthly rent with a deposit of 30 million won.
Michelle	It's more expensive than I thought.
Agent	Yes, it is quite expensive because it's close to the subway station.
Michelle	Well, when can I move in?
Agent	You can move in tomorrow. The previous tenant moved out last week, so nobody's there. Do you want to go take a look now?
Michelle	No, I'll talk to my friend first and then I'll be back.

Answers

(1) ②

Michelle went to a real estate agent to find a new apartment.

(2) ③

The apartment that the agent talked about has two bedrooms and a kitchen and its monthly rent is 500,000 won with a deposit of 30 million won. It is located near the school and there is a discount store nearby.

(3) ① 아니요 ② 네 ③ 아니요

This apartment is near the school. Also, anyone can move in right away since nobody is living there. But Michelle said she would come back after she has talked with her friend.

Vocabulary & Expression

장단점

장단점 means ***pros and cons***. 장단점 is an abbreviation of 장점 and 단점, meaning the pros and cons of a certain matter or thing.

ex A: 수잔 씨, 여행사에서 여러 사람이 같이 가는 단체 여행은 어때요?
B: 장단점이 있어요. 비용이 싸게 드니까 좋지만 모르는 사람들과 같이 가야 돼서 불편한 점도 있어요.

사생활을 간섭받아서

사생활을 간섭받아서 means ***because there is interference in one's private life.***

ex A: 그 하숙집은 어때요? 하숙집 아주머니가 친절하시죠?
B: 네. 그런데 가끔 사생활을 간섭받아서 힘들 때도 있어요.

Functional Expression

- **Saying that there is no need to prepare a meal**

When you want to say there is no need to prepare a meal, you can say 식사는 직접 준비하지 않아요, 식사 준비를 안 해도 돼요 or 식사 준비를 할 필요 없어요.

ex A: 하숙집에서는 제가 식사 준비를 해야 돼요?
B: 아니요. 식사는 직접 준비하지 않아요. /
수잔 씨가 식사 준비를 안 해도 돼요. /
수잔 씨가 식사 준비를 할 필요 없어요.

Dialogue

Michelle	Tien, you're living in a boarding house, right? Is it more convenient than living in the dormitory?
Tien	Well, there are pros and cons. But why are you asking? Do you want to move?
Michelle	Yes, I've been living in a dormitory but I'm going to move to a boarding house.
Tien	It's convenient to live in a boarding house since you don't have to prepare your own meals.
Michelle	Then what are the disadvantages of a boarding house?
Tien	Living in a boarding house can be inconvenient since there are many people living together, which means people often intrude on your private life.
Michelle	Really? It's comfortable to live in a dormitory since no one interferes with my life, but it's inconvenient in that I always have to eat out.
Tien	But can you make Korean friends if you live in a dormitory?
Michelle	You can, but it's hard to hang out with them since they are busy.
Tien	In a boarding house, you can easily make Korean friends because you meet them at mealtime.
Michelle	That sounds good. I should look for a good boarding house.

Grammar Focus

-게 되다 is used to show that the subject, contrary to his/her wishes or intentions, is put in a certain situation due to an external reason. It is only attached to a verb.

Basic form	-게 되다	Basic form	-게 되다
가다	가게 되다	살다	살게 되다
먹다	먹게 되다	듣다	듣게 되다
고르다	고르게 되다	짓다	짓게 되다

ex A: 요코 씨, 어디가 아파서 병원에 갔어요?
B: 병원에 가기 싫었는데 두통이 너무 심해서 가게 됐어요.

ex A: 티엔 씨, 어떻게 해서 운동을 시작하게 됐어요? 운동 안 좋아하잖아요.
B: 네, 운동은 정말 싫은데 몸이 안 좋아서 시작했어요.

ex A: 김민호 씨, 사장님과 오늘 같이 출근했어요?
B: 네. 사장님을 우연히 지하철역에서 만나서 같이 오게 됐어요.

ex A: 마이클 씨, 이 팝콘 좀 저쪽으로 옮겨 주세요.
B: 왜요? 팝콘이 맛이 없어요?
A: 아니요. 배가 고프지도 않은데 텔레비전을 보면서 자꾸 먹게 돼요.

ex A: 나타샤 씨, 어떻게 해서 한국에서 살게 됐어요?
B: 한국 남자와 결혼해서 여기에서 살게 됐어요.

ex A: 수잔 씨, 언제 그 소식을 들었어요?
B: 어제 우연히 친구한테서 듣게 되었어요.

Answers

① A: 왜 사무실을 옮겼어요?
B: 싸고 좋은 사무실을 구해서 옮기게 됐어요.

② A: 왜 면접시험을 급하게 봤어요?
B: 회사에서 갑자기 연락이 와서 보게 됐어요.

③ A: 왜 휴가에 여행을 못 갔어요?
B: 같이 가기로 한 사람들이 취소해서 못 가게 됐어요.

④ A: 왜 여자 친구하고 헤어졌어요?
B: 부모님이 만나는 걸 반대하셔서 헤어지게 됐어요.

⑤ A: 왜 아르바이트를 그만두었어요?
B: 회사에 취직이 돼서 아르바이트를 그만두게 됐어요.

02 • -(으)ㄹ수록

p.117

Grammar Focus

-(으)ㄹ수록 is used when as a situation or degree becomes more severe, the result or situation of the following clause also becomes proportionately stronger or weaker. To emphasize -(으)ㄹ수록, -(으)면 -(으)ㄹ수록 is used with the adjectives or verbs repeated.

Basic form	-(으)ㄹ수록	Basic form	-(으)ㄹ수록
많다	많을수록	먹다	먹을수록
덥다	더울수록	만들다	만들수록
멀다	멀수록	듣다	들을수록
가다	갈수록	돕다	도울수록

ex A: 그 하숙집은 시설도 별로 안 좋은데 값이 비싼 것 같아요.
B: 그 집은 바로 학교 앞에 있잖아요. 학교에서 가까울수록 찾는 사람이 많으니까 비싼 거죠.

ex A: 지금 여자 친구는 처음 봤을 때부터 마음에 들었어요?
B: 그건 아니에요. 그런데 여자 친구랑 말이 잘 통해서 만나면 만날수록 더 좋아하게 됐어요.

ex A: 아까부터 똑같은 노래를 계속 듣고 있군요. 그 노래 좋아요?
B: 네. 처음에 들었을 때는 그저 그랬는데 들을수록 괜찮은 거 같아요.

ex A: 수잔 씨가 만든 계란찜은 참 부드럽네요. 특별한 방법이 있어요?
B: 그거요? 계란을 풀어서 저을 때 여러 번 저으세요. 많이 저을수록 계란이 더 맛있어요.

ex A: 이 동네는 살기 편해요?
B: 네. 처음에는 몰랐는데 교통도 편하고 큰 슈퍼도 있고 해서 살면 살수록 전 여기가 좋아요.

Focus Plus

- 갈수록 has become an adverb, meaning 'more and more as time passes or things progress.'

ex A: 한국어 공부가 어때요?
B: 1급은 별로 어렵지 않았는데 2급은 좀 어려운 것 같아요. 갈수록 공부가 어려워요.

ex A: 새로 만난 반 친구들과 많이 친해요?
B: 네. 처음에는 서로 잘 몰라서 힘들었는데 갈수록 친하게 됐어요.

Answers

① 도와주는 사람이 많을수록 일이 빨리 끝나요.

② 한국말을 배울수록 재미있어서 계속 공부하게 돼요.

③ 한국 영화를 볼수록 한국 영화배우에 관심이 생겨요.

④ 학교에서 가까운 하숙집일수록 통학하기 편해서 찾는 사람이 많아요.

⑤ 아이들에게 영어를 가르칠수록 아이들 실력이 늘어서 보람이 있어요.

Vocabulary & Expression

신경을 써 주셔서

신경을 써 주셔서 means ***because (you) have been so considerate.*** It means because someone has been considerate even in trivial matters.

ex A: 연주회 초대장도 보내 주시고 신경을 써 주셔서 감사드립니다.
B: 별말씀을요. 저랑 가까운 분인데 꼭 와 주셔야죠.

텔레비전을 틀어요

텔레비전을 틀어요 means ***turn on the TV.*** It means to turn on the television so that it can be watched. 틀다 means to make electronic goods, such as sound equipment, run. It has the same meaning as 텔레비전을 켜다. 틀다 is used in such cases as 라디오를 틀다 or 에어컨을 틀다.

ex A: 뉴스 보고 싶은데 지금 텔레비전 좀 틀어요.
B: 네, 그럴게요.

방해가 되고

방해가 되고 means ***being interrupted.*** It indicates that a certain matter is interrupted and therefore ruined.

ex A: 왜 그렇게 조용히 방문을 닫고 나와요?
B: 마이클 씨가 공부하고 있는데 방해가 되면 안 되니까요.

잠도 자주 깨게 돼요

잠도 자주 깨게 돼요 means ***that (I) am often awakened from sleep.*** This expression means that one wants to keep sleeping but is often awakened because of disturbing sounds or other circumstances.

ex A: 왜 이렇게 계속 졸아요? 어제 잘 못 잤어요?
B: 네. 요즘 날씨가 너무 더워서 자다가 잠을 자주 깨게 돼요.

Functional Expression

- **To refuse in an indirect way**

Sometimes you may have to refuse another person's request in an indirect way. In such cases, you can say 그건 곤란해요, 그건 좀 어려운데요, 죄송하지만 그렇게는 안 돼요 or 죄송하지만 그건 좀 힘들겠어요 to be cautious and avoid giving offense.

ex A: 이 휴대 전화를 지난달에 샀어요. 그런데 색깔이 마음에 안 드는데 다른 걸로 바꿀 수 있나요?
B: 그건 곤란해요. /
그건 좀 어려운데요. /
죄송하지만 그렇게는 안 돼요. /
죄송하지만 그건 좀 힘들겠어요.

Script

Jan	Ma'am, I'd like to talk about something. Do you have time right now?
Ma'am	Yes, what's the matter? Please have a seat here.
Jan	The longer I live here, the more comfortable I feel since you have been so considerate in many ways.
Ma'am	Don't mention it. But what can I do for you?
Jan	I want to talk about the person living in the room next to mine. He always has the TV on loud at night. So it interrupts my study and often wakes me up at night. I am sorry but can you move me to another room?
Ma'am	I'm afraid that will be difficult. I will talk to him instead. He always comes late at night on weekdays so it's hard to catch him. I promise to talk to him this Saturday.
Jan	All right, please do so. I also want to talk about breakfast. I would like bread instead of rice. Could you prepare bread for breakfast?
Ma'am	Of course. That's no problem. Is there anything else bothering you?
Jan	No, everything else is good.
Ma'am	If there's anything you want, don't hesitate to ask me.

Answers

(1) ① 옆방에 사는 사람이 밤에 텔레비전을 항상 크게 튼다.
② 아침에 밥 대신에 빵을 먹고 싶다.
Jan is upset because the person living in the next room always keeps the TV on loud at night and because only rice is served for breakfast at the boarding house.

(2) ②
In regard to Jan's complaint, the boarding house keeper replied that she can't move Jan to another room, but would warn the person living next door and make bread available for breakfast.

(3) ① 아니요　② 네　③ 아니요
The person living in the next room comes late at night on weekdays but can be met on the weekend. Jan expressed his gratitude for the boarding house keeper's help and the boarding house keeper was not offended and told Jan to let her know if he had anything to ask her.

Vocabulary & Expression

간단한 건 전자레인지를 사용하면 돼요

간단한 건 전자레인지를 사용하면 돼요 means ***(you) can use a microwave to cook simple dishes.*** In this case, 간단한 건 means a dish that can be easily cooked, such as a precooked meal. Therefore, 간단한 건 전자레인지를 사용하면 돼요 means that one can use a microwave to cook a precooked meal or other easily prepared dish.

ex A: 이 기숙사에서는 음식은 어떻게 만들어 먹을 수 있어요?
B: 불을 사용하는 건 안 되지만 간단한 건 전자레인지를 사용하면 돼요.

Functional Expression

- **Asking if cooking is possible**

You can say 요리는 가능해요?, 요리할 수 있어요?, 요리해서 먹을 수 있어요? or 음식은 만들어서 먹을 수 있어요? to ask if cooking is possible when you stay in a hotel, guest house, or boarding house.

ex A: 여기에서 요리는 가능해요? /
여기에서 요리할 수 있어요? /
여기서 요리해서 먹을 수 있어요? /
여기서 음식은 만들어서 먹을 수 있어요?
B: 물론이죠. 가능합니다.

Dialogue

Lisa	How do you do? I'm Lisa, your roommate.
Eungyeong	Nice to meet you, Lisa. I'm Kim Eungyeong. I'm a senior majoring in politics. Where are you from, Lisa?
Lisa	I'm from America. I started studying Korean here this semester.
Eungyeong	Really? You speak Korean very well. Is it interesting to learn Korean?
Lisa	Yes, it's interesting, but the more I learn, the more difficult it becomes. By the way, what kind of facilities are available in this dormitory? Can we cook here?
Eungyeong	No, you can't cook but you can use a microwave for simple dishes. Also, there are many cafeterias at school so it won't be inconvenient.
Lisa	I see. Where is the laundry room?
Eungyeong	It's in the basement. There's a fitness room beside the laundry room and it's really well-equipped, so go check it out.
Lisa	Ok, I'll check it out tomorrow. Thank you.
Eungyeong	My pleasure. If there's anything you want to know, don't hesitate to ask me.

Vocabulary & Expression

저희 동네

저희 동네 means ***our neighborhood***. It means 우리 동네. 저희 is the lowered form of 우리, used when talking to someone older or a superior.

ex A: 수잔 씨, 사는 동네는 어때요? 살기 편해요?
B: 네. 저희 동네는 지하철역도 있어서 살기 아주 편해요.

ex A: 왕카이 씨 아니에요? 저희 동네에는 어쩐 일이세요?
B: 아, 나타샤 씨. 친구가 이 근처에 살아서 놀러 왔어요.

마음을 정하지 못했는데

마음을 정하지 못했는데 means ***but (I) haven't made up my mind***. It means that one has not decided what to do or what to choose among a number of options.

ex A: 티엔 씨, 어느 대학교에 갈 거예요? 결정했어요?
B: 아니요. 아직 마음을 정하지 못했는데 장학금을 주는 곳으로 갈 것 같아요.

Functional Expression

- **Telling people to leave a reply for inquiries**

To tell others who have read your post on the Internet to leave a reply if they have questions or inquiries, you can use expressions such as 궁금한 게 있으면 글을 올려 주세요, 물어볼 게 있으면 답글을 남겨 주세요, 궁금하신 게 있으시면 댓글을 써 주세요 or 더 알고 싶은 게 있으시면 제 글에 답글을 달아 주세요.

ex 궁금한 게 있으면 글을 올려 주세요. /
물어볼 게 있으면 답글을 남겨 주세요. /
궁금하신 게 있으시면 댓글을 써 주세요. /
더 알고 싶은 게 있으시면 다시 제 글에 답글을 달아 주세요.

Pronunciation

Weakened ㅎ

ㅎ is pronounced softly between a vowel and another vowel or between final consonants ㄴ, ㅁ, ㅇ, ㄹ and a vowel. In this case, the final consonants ㄴ, ㅁ, ㅇ, ㄹ should be pronounced as soft consonants.

ex 결혼한[결혼한], [겨로난], 불편했습니다[불편핻씀니다], [불펴낻씀니다], 편합니다[편함니다], [펴남니다], 편해서[편해서], [펴내서], 이동할[이동할].[이동알], 시원한[시원한], [시워난], 궁금한[궁금한], [궁그만]

Text

Q I want to move to Yeouido. Is it a convenient place to live?

Seoul Person, October 20

A Yeouido is really good. Come to Yeouido.

Black Star, October 21

Hello.

I'm Black Star and I have been living in Yeouido for 10 years. I moved to Yeouido when I was in university and I settled here even after I got married because of my work. When I first moved here, it was inconvenient because there was no big supermarket or department store. But the longer I live here, the more convenient it becomes, as a discount store has opened up recently and there is a department store nearby.

In my neighborhood, there are more offices than apartments. But it is not crowded on the weekend as most of the offices are closed. The transportation is also convenient, so it is easy to go to the south or north side of the river by subway and bus.

Moreover, you can enjoy the four seasons in Yeouido Park and Hangang Park. You can enjoy fireworks and cherry blossoms in spring, cool fountains in summer, beautiful colored leaves in autumn, and snow on the river in winter. Please leave a message if you have more questions about Yeouido.

↳ I haven't made up my mind, but I think I should move to Yeouido. Thank you, Black Star.

Seoul Person, October 20

Answers

(1) ②, ④, ⑤

The good points of this neighborhood include the convenient transportation, a recently opened discount store that makes shopping easy, and the fact that weekends are not crowded because the offices are closed.

(2) ① 아니요　② 아니요　③ 네

Black Star moved to Yeouido when he/she was in university. One can enjoy the four seasons in Yeouido even though there are no particular festivals. Also, the person who asked the question is likely to move to Yeouido, because that's what he/she said in the last reply.

(3) 이 동네는 교통도 편해서 강남이나 강북으로 갈 때 지하철, 버스로 쉽게 이동할 수 있습니다. 그리고 여의도공원과 한강시민공원이 있어서 사계절을 즐길 수 있습니다. 봄에는 불꽃놀이, 벚꽃놀이, 여름에는 시원한 분수, 가을에는 공원의 멋진 단풍, 겨울에는 한강에 내리는 눈을 볼 수 있습니다.

Vocabulary Check

▶ **Tick off the words and expressions that you know.**

기숙사 시설	**Dormitory Facilities**
☐ 1인 1실	single room
☐ 2인 1실	twin room
☐ 세탁실	laundry room
☐ 조리실	kitchen
☐ 경비실	doorman's office
☐ 체력 단련실	fitness room, gym
☐ 공동 샤워실	common shower room
☐ 냉방 시설	air-conditioning
☐ 난방 시설	heating system
☐ 휴게실	lounge

이사할 집과 이사 준비	**A New House to Move and the Preparation for Moving**
☐ 개인 샤워실이 있다	to have a private shower booth
☐ 공동 샤워실을 쓰다	to use a public shower booth
☐ 교육 환경이 좋다	to have a good education environment
☐ 교통이 편리하다	to be convenient for transportation
☐ 물건을 사기 편하다	to be convenient for shopping
☐ 방값을 물어보다	to ask the price of a room
☐ 부동산 소개소에 가다	to go to a real estate agency
☐ 사생활을 간섭 받다	to have one's private life intruded upon
☐ 사생활을 간섭하다	to intrude on someone's private life
☐ 새로 이사할 곳을 알아보다	to look for a place to move to
☐ 시설이 좋다	to be well-equipped
☐ 식사 준비를 직접 하다	to prepare a meal by oneself
☐ 인터넷이 되다	to have access to the Internet
☐ 조리 시설이 있다	to have cooking facilities
☐ 주변 자연 환경이 좋다	to have a good surrounding natural environment
☐ 주변에 편의시설이 있다	to have amenities nearby
☐ 주변이 조용하다	to have quiet surroundings
☐ 통학하기 편하다	to be convenient for commuting
☐ 하숙집을 구하다	to look for a boarding house
☐ 학교 근처로 옮기다	to move to a place near school
☐ 학교/회사에서 가깝다	to be close to school/ the office
☐ 학교/회사에서 멀다	to be far from school/ the office
☐ 한 방을 쓰다	to share a room

이웃	**Neighbors**
☐ 같은 방 친구	roommate
☐ 동네 사람	neighbor/ person living in the same neighborhood
☐ 아래층 사람	person living downstairs
☐ 옆집 사람	person living next door/ next-door neighbor
☐ 집 주인	owner of a house
☐ 이웃 사람	neighbor

PART1 준비합시다 01 • -(으)ㄹ까 하다

p.128

Grammar Focus

-(으)ㄹ까 하다 is used to talk about a vague idea or plan that is quite possible to put into action, even though nothing has been decided for certain. It is attached to a verb, and if the verb stem ends in a consonant -을까 하다 is used, while -ㄹ까 하다 is used if it ends in the consonant ㄹ or a vowel.

Basic form	-(으)ㄹ까 하다	Basic form	-(으)ㄹ까 하다
가다	갈까 하다	열다	열까 하다
자르다	자를까 하다	돕다	도울까 하다
먹다	먹을까 하다	듣다	들을까 하다
읽다	읽을까 하다	짓다	지을까 하다

ex A: 저녁에 뭐 먹을 거예요?
B: 비빔밥을 먹을까 해요. 요코 씨가 맛있는 식당을 가르쳐 줬거든요.

ex A: 티엔 씨 생일 선물로 뭘 줄 거예요?
B: 글쎄요. 저는 케이크를 만들까 해요. 좀 특별한 선물을 주고 싶거든요.

ex A: 오늘 수업이 끝난 후에 뭐 할 거예요?
B: 집에서 한국어 CD를 들을까 해요. 내일 시험이거든요.

Focus Plus

- Just like -(으)ㄹ까 하다, -(으)ㄹ 거예요 (See 「이화 한국어 1-2」 Chapter 9, p.37) and -(으)려고 하다 (See 「이화 한국어 1-2」 Chapter 11, p.72) are also used when talking about plans, but they express a stronger sense of determination than -(으)ㄹ까 하다 or are used when a plan is about to be put into action.

ex A: 주말에 뭐 할 거예요?
B: 요즘 많이 피곤해요. 그래서 집에서 푹 쉬려고 해요.

Answers

① A: 소피 씨, 이번 방학에 뭘 할 거예요?
B: 운전면허를 딸까 해요. 서울에서 운전을 하고 싶거든요.

② A: 장소이 씨, 이번 방학에 뭘 할 거예요?
B: 도자기를 만들까 해요. 친구에게 선물하려고 하거든요.

③ A: 티엔 씨, 이번 방학에 뭘 할 거예요?
B: 한국 시집을 읽을까 해요. 시에 관심이 생겼거든요.

④ A: 미셸 씨, 이번 방학에 뭘 할 거예요?
B: 아르바이트를 할까 해요. 좋은 하숙집으로 이사하고 싶거든요.

⑤ A: 왕카이 씨, 이번 방학에 뭘 할 거예요?
B: 악기 동아리에 가입할까 해요. 요즘 기타를 배우고 있거든요.

Grammar Focus

-(으)ㄴ/는/(으)ㄹ 모양이다 is used to fathom a situation based on the surrounding circumstances or atmosphere. It is attached to an adjective or a verb. -(으)ㄴ 모양이다 can be used with an adjective, and -(으)ㄴ/는/(으)ㄹ 모양이다 with a verb when making presumptions about past, present, and future situations.

Basic form	-(으)ㄴ 모양이다	-는 모양이다	-(으)ㄹ 모양이다
크다	큰 모양이다	-	-
힘들다	힘든 모양이다	-	-
가다	간 모양이다	가는 모양이다	갈 모양이다
읽다	읽은 모양이다	읽는 모양이다	읽을 모양이다
돕다	도운 모양이다	돕는 모양이다	도울 모양이다
듣다	들은 모양이다	듣는 모양이다	들을 모양이다
짓다	지은 모양이다	짓는 모양이다	지을 모양이다
학생이다	학생인 모양이다	-	-

ex A: 마이클 씨는 요즘 주말에도 회사에 가요.
B: 일이 많아서 바쁜 모양이에요.

ex A: 나타샤 씨가 아까부터 전화만 보고 있어요.
B: 친구의 연락을 기다리는 모양이에요.

ex A: 요코 씨가 성적표를 보면서 웃고 있어요.
B: 시험을 잘 본 모양이에요.

ex A: 하늘에 구름이 많아요.
B: 비가 올 모양이에요.

Focus Plus

- -(으)ㄴ/는/(으)ㄹ 모양이다 is used to roughly estimate circumstances based on the surrounding conditions. Therefore, when talking about one's experience but without much confidence, -(으)ㄴ/는/(으)ㄹ 것 같다 (See 『이화 한국어 2-1』 Chapter 7, p.129) should be used instead of -(으)ㄴ/는/(으)ㄹ 모양이다.

ex 어제 프랑크가 본 영화가 아주 재미있는 것 같아요. (○)
어제 프랑크가 본 영화가 아주 재미있는 모양이에요. (○)
어제 제가 본 영화가 아주 재미있는 것 같아요. (○)
어제 제가 본 영화가 아주 재미있는 모양이에요. (×)

Answers

① 두 남자가 음식을 먹지 않고 이야기만 하고 있어요. 음식을 다 먹은 모양이에요.

② 남자가 혼자 앉아서 시계를 보고 있어요. 친구를 기다리는 모양이에요.

③ 남자가 여자에게 선물을 주고 있어요. 여자 친구의 생일인 모양이에요.

Vocabulary & Expression

만석입니다

만석입니다 means that ***all seats are booked.*** To say that all tickets have been sold, 매진 can be used instead of 만석.

ex A: 공연장에 빈자리가 없네요.
B: 네, 오늘 공연도 만석이에요. 정말 인기가 많네요.

ex A: 이번 주말에 부산으로 가는 기차표를 예매하고 싶은데요.
B: 손님, 이번 주말 부산행 기차표는 모두 매진입니다.

대기자 명단에 올려 주시고

대기자 명단에 올려 주시고 means ***put (me) on the waiting list***. 명단에 올리다 is to write the name of a person who wants to sign up for something on the list.

ex A: (음식점에서) 손님, 지금 자리가 없습니다. 기다리시겠습니까?
B: 네. 그럼 대기자 명단에 올려 주시고 빈자리가 생기면 불러 주세요.

ex A: 이번 봉사 활동에 참여하고 싶은데요.
B: 네. 그럼 명단에 이름을 올려 드릴게요.

전화와 문자로 연락이 갈 겁니다

전화와 문자로 연락이 갈 겁니다 means ***(you) will receive a call and a text message***. It means that when a person needs to be contacted, he/she will receive a call and a text message. When talking about the method of contacting a person, you can say N(으)로 연락이 가다. When 말, 소식, 연락, or 결과 comes in front of 가다, this indicates that a message or news will be sent.

ex A: 물건을 배달해 주실 때 먼저 연락을 주시지요?
B: 그럼요. 고객님께 먼저 전화와 문자로 연락이 갈 겁니다.

ex A: 면접에서 합격하면 연락을 주시나요?
B: 네, 이메일로 결과가 갈 거예요.

Functional Expression

- **Saying that a booking is possible**

  When telling customers reservations can be made at a train station, cinema, or other place, the expressions 자리가 있습니다, 예매 가능합니다, 아직 표가 있습니다 can be used.

ex A: 저녁 8시 영화를 예매하려고 하는데요.
B: 네, 자리가 있습니다. / 네, 예매 가능합니다. /
네, 아직 표가 있습니다. / 네, 예매하실 수 있습니다.

- **Saying farewell to a guest**

  When saying goodbye to customers in a store or institution such as a post office or bank, the expressions 좋은 하루 되세요, 즐거운 하루 보내세요, 오늘 하루 즐겁게 보내세요 etc. can be used. These expressions are also suitable as a fairly formal closing for an email or text message.

  ex A: 손님, 좋은 하루 되세요. / 손님, 즐거운 하루 보내세요. / 손님, 오늘 하루 즐겁게 보내세요.
  B: 감사합니다.

Script

Staff	Ewha Airlines. How may I help you?
Michelle	I'd like to book a flight to New York on September 4.
Staff	I'm sorry, but all the flights to New York on that day are fully booked. If it's alright for you to leave on September 10, we have seats available then.
Michelle	Really?
Staff	And after September 6, the rates go down a little too. Would you like a seat for September 10?
Michelle	Yes, and I also need to make a reservation for a return fight, either on September 25 or 26.
Staff	I'm sorry but no seats are available on those two days.
Michelle	I guess there are no seats because it's the weekend. Then how about the 24th, a Friday?
Staff	Yes, we do have some seats left.
Michelle	Then can you put me on the waiting list for the 25th and make a reservation for September 24?
Staff	Alright. If anybody cancels a return flight on the 25th, we'll give you a call and send you a text message as well.
Michelle	Okay, thank you.
Staff	Your reservation is complete for a round-trip ticket from Seoul to New York on September 10 and returning on September 24. Your reservation number is 7789. Have a nice day.

Answers

(1) ③ Michelle wanted to reserve a ticket for September 4, but since all the tickets were sold she booked a flight for September 10.

(2) ③

(3) ① 네 ② 네 ③ 아니요
Tickets after September 6 are cheaper than on the 4th. When there is a cancellation, the airline will make a call and send a text message to a person on the waiting list. Michelle made a reservation for a return flight and also asked that her name be placed on the waiting list.

Vocabulary & Expression

성함

성함 is the honorific form of 이름(name). 존함 can be used instead when referring to the name of someone older or superior.

ex A: 예약하신 분 성함이 어떻게 되세요?
B: 김민수인데요.

Functional Expression

- **Asking and answering if free parking is available**

When you ask if free parking is permitted, you can say 무료 주차가 됩니까? 무료로 주차할 수 있습니까? 주차장을 무료로 이용할 수 있습니까? etc. If free parking is allowed, you can say 주차는 1시간 동안 무료입니다, 주차장을 무료로 이용할 수 있습니다, 1시간 동안 무료로 주차할 수 있습니다, etc.

ex A: 무료 주차가 됩니까? / 무료로 주차할 수 있습니까? / 주차장을 무료로 이용할 수 있습니까?
B: 네, 주차는 1시간 동안 무료입니다. / 네, 주차장을 무료로 이용할 수 있습니다. / 네, 1시간 동안 무료로 주차할 수 있습니다. / 네, 물건을 산 영수증이 있으면 1시간 무료 주차가 가능합니다.

Dialogue

Staff	Ewha Buffet. How may I help you?
Natasha	I'd like to confirm my reservation for next Wednesday at 6 o'clock.
Staff	Whose name did you use to book a room?
Natasha	It's under Natasha.
Staff	(after a while) I am sorry, I cannot find the name on the reservation list.
Natasha	Then could you look for Ewha Photography Club? My friend might have made a reservation under a different name.
Staff	Yes, here it is. Five in your party, right?
Natasha	Yes, but we have a friend whose birthday is on that day. Could you provide a birthday cake by any chance?
Staff	If you notify us in advance, we'll prepare a cake free of charge.
Natasha	Then could you please arrange that for us.
Staff	Then let me just confirm your reservation. Five people at 6 pm on Wednesday the 9th.
Natasha	Thank you. I'm thinking of bringing my car that day. How long can I park there?
Staff	We give you a three-hour parking permit. When you pay at the counter, you can show our staff the parking ticket and he/she will stamp it.
Natasha	I see. Thank you.

Grammar Focus

-(으)ㄹ 줄 알다 is used to say you know how to do something. When you do not know how, you can say -(으)ㄹ 줄 모르다. It is attached to a verb, and -을 줄 알다 is used if the verb stem ends in a consonant, while -ㄹ 줄 알다 is used if it ends in the consonant ㄹ or a vowel.

Basic form	-(으)ㄹ 줄 알다/모르다	Basic form	-(으)ㄹ 줄 알다/모르다
타다	탈 줄 알다/모르다	듣다	들을 줄 알다/모르다
자르다	자를 줄 알다/모르다	만들다	만들 줄 알다/ 모르다
먹다	먹을 줄 알다/모르다	돕다	도울 줄 알다/모르다
읽다	읽을 줄 알다/모르다	짓다	지을 줄 알다/모르다

ex A: 수영할 줄 알아요?
B: 네, 할 줄 알아요. 어렸을 때 아버지께서 가르쳐 주셨어요.

ex A: 요즘 유행하는 춤을 출 줄 알아요?
B: 아니요, 출 줄 몰라요. 민수 씨가 좀 가르쳐 주세요.

ex A: 김치찌개를 만들 줄 알아요?
B: 네, 만들 줄 알아요. 지난주에 요리 교실에서 배웠어요.

Focus Plus

- -(으)ㄹ 수 있다/없다 (See 『이화 한국어 1-2』 Chapter 14, p.114) is used when you know or don't know how to do something just like -(으)ㄹ 줄 알다/모르다. However, -(으)ㄹ 수 있다/없다 is also used to indicate whether doing a certain thing is possible or not.

  ex 저는 운전할 줄 알아요. 그렇지만 지금 술을 마셔서 운전할 수 없어요.

Answers

① A: 마이클 씨, 국제 전화를 걸 줄 알아요?
B: 아니요. 몰라요. 티엔 씨는요?
A: 저는 걸 줄 알아요.

② A: 마이클 씨, 홈페이지를 만들 줄 알아요?
B: 네. 알아요. 티엔 씨는요?
A: 저는 만들 줄 몰라요.

③ A: 마이클 씨, 현금 인출기를 사용할 줄 알아요?
B: 네. 알아요. 티엔 씨는요?
A: 저도 사용할 줄 알아요.

④ A: 마이클 씨, 인터넷으로 물건을 살 줄 알아요?
B: 아니요. 몰라요. 티엔 씨는요?
A: 저도 살 줄 몰라요.

⑤ A: 마이클 씨, 수동 카메라로 사진을 찍을 줄 알아요?
B: 아니요. 몰라요. 티엔 씨는요?
A: 저는 찍을 줄 알아요.

Grammar Focus

When -(으)ㄴ/는 대신(에) is attached to an adjective, it indicates that the state of the previous clause is different to that of the following clause. When attached to a verb, it indicates that the action in the previous clause is replaced with some other action or an equivalent action to compensate. -(으)ㄴ 대신(에) can be used with an adjective, -(으)ㄴ 대신(에) with a past tense verb, and -는 대신(에) with a present tense verb.

Basic form	-(으)ㄴ 대신에	Basic form	-(으)ㄴ 대신에	-는 대신에
싸다	싼 대신에	보다	본 대신에	보는 대신에
넓다	넓은 대신에	읽다	읽은 대신에	읽는 대신에
멀다	먼 대신에	듣다	들은 대신에	듣는 대신에
어렵다	어려운 대신에	젓다	저은 대신에	젓는 대신에

ex A: 사과가 한 개에 1,500원이에요? 너무 비싼 거 아니에요?
B: 비싼 대신에 품질이 아주 좋아요.

ex A: 티엔 씨, 왜 이렇게 늦게 왔어요?
B: 미안해요. 제가 늦은 대신에 오늘은 밥을 살게요.

ex A: 내일 이사하지요? 제가 좀 도와줄까요?
B: 네, 고마워요. 이사를 도와주는 대신에 맛있는 음식을 만들어 줄게요.

ex A: 식사했어요?
B: 아니요. 늦게 일어나서 밥을 먹는 대신에 우유 한 잔 마셨어요.

ex A: 이 소설책 정말 재미있어요. 다 읽은 후에 빌려 줄게요.
B: 좋아요. 책을 빌려 주는 대신에 제가 커피 살게요.

Answers

① A: 벌써 여행을 예약했어요?
B: 네. 미리 예약한 대신에 할인을 받았어요.

② A: 그 집은 교통이 편리해요?
B: 네. 교통이 편리한 대신에 월세가 비싸요.

③ A: 1년 동안 장학금을 받기로 했어요?
B: 네. 장학금을 받는 대신에 성적을 잘 받아야 해요.

④ A: 아버지 생신에 선물을 안 보냈어요?
B: 네. 선물을 하지 않은 대신에 어머니와 여행을 보내 드릴 거예요.

⑤ A: 친구들에게 일본어를 가르쳐 줘요?
B: 네. 일본어를 알려 주는 대신에 친구들한테서 한국어를 배워요.

Grammar Focus

-던 is used when you are reminded of and talk about a situation, action, or a repeated action that was not completed but was still ongoing in the past. It is attached to an adjective or a verb whether the stem of the adjective or verb ends in a consonant or a vowel. A noun follows, since a phrase containing -던 is used like an adjectival clause.

Basic form	-던	Basic form	-던
싸다	싸던	보다	보던
넓다	넓던	읽다	읽던
멀다	멀던	듣다	듣던
어렵다	어렵던	젓다	젓던

ex A: 이 노래 기억나요?
B: 당연하지요. 작년 여름에 인기가 많던 노래잖아요.

ex A: 제가 마시던 우유는 어디에 있어요?
B: 미안해요. 다 마신 거 아니었어요? 모르고 제가 버렸어요.

ex A: 아까 여기에서 울던 아이가 어디로 갔어요?
B: 아이 엄마가 와서 집으로 데려 갔어요.

Focus Plus

- -(으)ㄴ (See 「이화 한국어 1-2」 Chapter 15, p.131) is also used to talk about what happened in the past. However, only -던 can be used to talk about something that was continuing in the past, was stopped in the middle, or still had a possibility of taking place again.

  ex 어제 먹던 밥이 지금 어디에 있지? (○)
  어제 먹은 밥이 지금 어디에 있지? (×)

Answers

① A: 고향에 있을 때 어떤 동네에 살았습니까?
B: 제가 살던 동네는 작은 시골 마을입니다. 조용하고 예쁜 곳이었어요.

② A: 고향에서 무슨 운동을 주로 했습니까?
B: 제가 주로 하던 운동은 한국 사람도 좋아하는 축구입니다. 재미있었어요.

③ A: 고향에서 무슨 음악을 자주 들었습니까?
B: 제가 자주 듣던 음악은 비틀즈의 'Yesterday'입니다. 가사가 좋았어요.

④ A: 고향에서 아프면 어느 병원에 자주 갔습니까?
B: 제가 자주 가던 병원은 집에서 가까운 병원입니다. 친절한 곳이었어요.

⑤ A: 고향에서 가족들과 무슨 음식을 자주 만들어 먹었습니까?
B: 제가 가족들과 자주 만들어 먹던 음식은 토마토와 계란이 들어 있는 샌드위치입니다. 정말 맛있었어요.

Vocabulary & Expression

한동안

한동안 means ***for quite a long time.***

ex A: 우표가 왜 이렇게 많아요?
B: 제 취미가 우표 모으기라서 제가 한동안 모았던 거예요.

ex A: 왜 이렇게 전화를 안 받아요?
B: 미안해요. 너무 피곤해서 한동안 책상에 앉아서 졸았어요.

치수

치수 means ***size, measure.*** It refers to the size of clothing or an object. For example, 90(S), 95(M), 100(L), 105(XL) are sizes for T-shirts and shirts and 55(S), 66(M), 77(L) for women's clothes in Korea.

ex A: 이거 저한테 작을 것 같은데 혹시 한 치수 큰 것도 있어요?
B: 죄송합니다, 손님. 이게 가장 큰 치수예요.

ex A: 이 재킷을 입어 보고 싶은데 어떤 치수가 저한테 맞을까요??
B: 손님은 55 입으시면 돼요.

Functional Expression

- **Talking about a popular product**
  To say something is popular, N이/가 잘 팔려요, N이/가 유행이에요, N을/를 많이 찾아요, and N이/가 인기가 많아요 can be used.

  ex A: 요즘 학생들에게 어떤 운동화가 인기가 많아요?
  B: 화려한 색깔 운동화가 잘 팔려요. /
  화려한 색깔 운동화가 유행이에요. /
  화려한 색깔 운동화를 많이 찾아요. /
  화려한 색깔 운동화가 인기가 많아요.

- **Asking for a discount**
  When the price seems expensive and you want the salesperson to cut down the price, you can say 좀 깎아 주세요, 좀 싸게 해 주세요, 좀 깎아 주시면 안 돼요?

  ex A: 이 티셔츠는 오만 원이에요.
  B: 좀 깎아 주세요. /
  좀 싸게 해 주세요. /
  좀 깎아 주시면 안 돼요? /
  좀 싸게 해 주실 수 없어요?

Script

Sales clerk	How are you? How can I help you?
Zhang Souyi	I'd like to buy a Korean *hanbok*.
Sales clerk	Ah, when are you going to wear it?
Zhang Souyi	There's an event at school and I'm going to wear it then.
Sales clerk	I see. People tend to like fancy designs these days. How about this one?
Zhang Souyi	Well, it's a bit too fancy.
Sales clerk	Then how about this one? This design is still popular but for a long time it was very sought after. The price is 200,000 won. The one I showed you before is 240,000 won.
Zhang Souyi	Can't you cut the price a little?
Sales clerk	This is not expensive at all. Instead of lowering the price, I'll give you a headpiece that goes well with the *hanbok*.
Zhang Souyi	Okay, then can I try it on?
Sales clerk	Of course. Do you know how to put it on? You put on the skirt first and then the jacket. Come out when you've changed. I'll help you with other stuff. The fitting room's over there. (after changing into the *hanbok*)
Zhang Souyi	The sleeves and the skirt are a little bit short. I need one size bigger.
Sales clerk	You'll have to make a special order for a bigger size. If we place an order today, you'll get it in about three days.
Zhang Souyi	Okay. Then I'll place an order for one size bigger.
Sales clerk	Alright. I will do that then.

Answers

(1) 학교에서 행사가 있어서 그때 입으려고 한다.

(2) ②
The sleeves and skirt of the *hanbok* that Zhang Souyi is wearing right now are a little short.

(3) ① 아니요 ② 아니요 ③ 아니요
The *hanbok* that Zhang Souyi has picked is still popular these days but was very popular in the past as well. It is not certain whether Zhang Souyi has ever tried on *hanbok* before, but the clerk told her how to wear it and helped her put it on. The clerk did not cut the price but gave her a free headpiece instead.

Vocabulary & Expression

서두르시는 게 좋을 겁니다

서두르시는 게 좋을 겁니다 means ***(you) should hurry***. It indicates that you should move faster than before. 서두르다 means to hurry and move quickly so that something can be done in time or sooner than expected.

ex A: 영화 표를 몇 시로 예매했어요?
B: 7시요. 10분 남았어요. 늦지 않으려면 서두르시는 게 좋을 거예요.

Functional Expression

- **Asking when an out-of-stock item will be available again**

  When asking when an out-of-stock item will be available again, you can say 언제 다시 들어와요?, 언제부터 다시 팔아요?, 언제쯤 다시 구입할 수 있어요? etc.

  ex A: 파란색 가방은 언제 다시 들어와요? /
  파란색 가방은 언제부터 다시 팔아요? /
  파란색 가방을 언제쯤 다시 구입할 수 있어요?
  B: 다음 주 화요일요.

Dialogue

Clerk Ewha Bookstore. What can I do for you?
Tien I'd like to place an order for a book. Do you have the books titled *Korean Food Tour* and *Inseo Park's Movie Walk*?
Clerk Just a minute. (after a minute) We have *Movie Walk* but *Korean Food Tour* is out of stock.
Tien Really? Then I'd like to have *Movie Walk* delivered. The address is Seodaemun-gu, Daehyun-dong, Ewha Residence Hall, Room 105.
Clerk I got it. If I send it out today, you will probably get it the day after tomorrow.
Tien The day after tomorrow? I need the book tomorrow. Could you send it by overnight delivery? I'll pay the additional cost.
Clerk Alright. Then the book is 15,000 won, plus an additional 2,000 won. That's 17,000 won altogether. You can put the money in our account.
Tien Okay. And when do you expect *Korean Food Tour* to be in stock again?
Clerk Next Monday. But we will be taking advance orders on the Internet from this Friday.
Tien I don't know how to make an order on the Internet. Can I do it on the phone?
Clerk Then call us Friday morning. The book has been selling very well since last year so you should hurry.
Tien I see. I will give you a call then.

Vocabulary & Expression

예매에 얽힌 일화

예매에 얽힌 일화 means ***funny stories about making reservations.*** 얽히다 means to be related to something in some way. It is generally used in the form of N에 얽히다 or N와/과 얽히다.

ex A: 뭘 그렇게 재미있게 듣고 있어요?
B: 민수 씨가 비행기 표 예매에 얽힌 일화를 말하고 있는데 정말 재미있어요.

착각을 해서

착각을 해서 means ***because (I) made a mistake.*** 착각하다 is to mistake some fact or object for something else. It is generally used in the form of N을/를 N(으)로 착각하다.

ex A: 왜 이렇게 늦었어요?
B: 미안해요. 약속 시간을 착각해서 집에서 늦게 나왔어요.

ex A: 저 배우는 여자예요?
B: 네, 여자예요. 머리가 짧고 목소리가 낮아서 저도 처음에는 남자로 착각했어요.

사람들 사이를 뚫고

사람들 사이를 뚫고 means ***forging through a crowd of people.*** This expression refers to pushing ahead through a group of people blocking the way. Here 뚫다 means to forge through an obstacle. It is usually used in the form of N을/를 뚫다 to indicate removal of an obstacle or overcoming a difficulty.

ex A: 출근 시간에는 지하철에 사람들이 너무 많아요.
B: 맞아요. 그래서 항상 사람들 사이를 뚫고 어렵게 지하철을 타요.

ex A: 가고 싶었던 대학교에 합격했어요.
B: 정말 축하해요. 높은 경쟁률을 뚫고 합격했군요.

Pronunciation

Intonation

Identifying meaning by using pitch variation is called 'intonation.' You should lower the ending in a declarative sentence and raise the ending in an interrogative sentence. To emphasize a word, the pitch should be raised a bit higher.

직원 : "손님이 예약하신 영화는 11시에 시작하는 겁니다. 상영 시간이 지나서 들어갈 수 없습니다."
남자 : "네? 뭐라고요?"
여자 : "어떻게 그걸 모를 수 있어요? 그리고 30분이나 걸어왔는데 이게 뭐예요?"

Text

An Embarrassing Mistake

Ⓐ When I go to see a movie or a concert, I always make a reservation. Making a reservation means I can pick the time I want. But sometimes I make a mistake and make the wrong reservation.

Ⓑ When we got to the front of the cinema, there was a crowd of people who wanted to buy tickets at the box office. My girlfriend was very happy and said, "The movie must be a lot of fun." I was pleased too. We worked our way through the crowd to the box office at the entrance.

Ⓒ Then, I showed the reservation number at the ticketing booth. But the person in the booth said to me, "You made a reservation for the 11 o'clock movie. It's already finished so you can't go in." Then she told me to leave. I was so surprised and said, "What? What did you say?" and checked my reservation. It was really for the 11 o'clock movie. By mistake I had made a reservation for 11 o'clock, thinking it was for 2 o'clock. My girlfriend said to me, "How could you not realize that? And we walked 30 minutes all the way down here for this? What now?" I had nothing to say. It was such an embarrassing day.

Ⓓ On the day, I met my girlfriend at a restaurant. Over lunch, I talked about when I went to school, and when I was learning Korean before coming to Korea to study. After lunch, we walked all the way to the theatre talking instead of taking the bus.

Ⓔ I was introduced to a Korean girl a few months ago. One day I decided to watch a movie with my girlfriend, so I planned to book the tickets in advance. However, I could only book online, so I asked a friend who's good with computers to do it for me and got the reservation number from him. I was going to book for an 11 o'clock movie but then I thought we should have lunch first, so I ended up making a reservation for a 2 o'clock movie.

Answers

(1) (A) → (E) → (D) → (B) → (C)

(2) ②, ③, ⑤

The man was introduced to a Korean woman a few months ago and when the two went to a movie theatre, the box office employee told them that since the movie was over they could not go in.

(3) 남자가 11시 영화를 예매했는데 2시로 착각해서 영화를 볼 수 없었다.

Vocabulary Check

▶ **Tick off the words and expressions that you know.**

비행기에서	In the Plane
☐ 1등석에 앉다	to fly first class
☐ 기내식을 먹다	to eat an in-flight meal
☐ 뉴욕행	to New York
☐ 대기자 명단에 올리다	to put somebody on the waiting list
☐ 만석이다	to be fully booked
☐ 비행기 좌석이 생기다	to have a seat made available
☐ 비행기에 탑승하다	to board the plane
☐ 비행기에서 내리다	to get off the plane
☐ 비행기 표를 확인하다	to check one's plane ticket
☐ 안전벨트를 매다	to put on one's seat belt
☐ 예약을 취소하다	to cancel a reservation
☐ 왕복	round-trip
☐ 인천발	from Incheon
☐ 일반석에 앉다	to fly economy class
☐ 자리가 있다	to have seats available
☐ 창가 자리를 예약하다	to reserve a window seat
☐ 통로 자리에 앉다	to sit in an aisle seat
☐ 편도	one-way
☐ 휴대 전화를 끄다	to turn off one's cell phone

영화관에서	At the Cinema
☐ 관람객이 많다	to have a large audience
☐ 매표소에서 표를 사다	to buy a ticket at the box office
☐ 상영 시간이 되다	to be the start of screening time
☐ 영화관 입구에 줄을 서다	to line up at the cinema entrance
☐ 영화를 관람하다	to see a movie
☐ 예약 번호를 보여 주다	to show one's reservation number
☐ 팝콘을 사다	to buy popcorn

예약과 주문	Reservations and Orders
☐ 남은 게 없다	to have nothing left
☐ 매진이다	to be sold out
☐ 물건을 사다	to buy a product
☐ 물건을 착각하다	to mistake an object for something else
☐ 미리 예약하다	to book in advance
☐ 서비스로 받다	to receive for free
☐ 예매하다	to reserve
☐ 예약 방법을 알다	to know how to make a reservation
☐ 예약 번호를 받다	to receive a reservation number
☐ 예약자 이름을 알다	to know the name of the person who made the booking
☐ 예약하다	to reserve, to make a booking
☐ 예약한 사람 이름을 말하다	to give the name of the person who made the booking
☐ 인터넷으로 주문하다	to order online
☐ 재고가 없다	to not have in stock
☐ 재고가 있다	to have in stock
☐ 전부 다 팔리다	to sell out
☐ 주문 예약을 받다	to take advance orders
☐ 주문하다	to order
☐ 퀵 서비스로 배달하다	to deliver by motorcycle courier
☐ 택배비를 계좌로 보내다	to put the delivery fee into the bank account
☐ 택배로 보내다	to send by courier
☐ 품절되다	to be sold out
☐ 할인 판매하다	to sell at a discount
☐ 현금으로 계산하다	to pay in cash

 p.146

Grammar Focus

–았/었었– is used when a certain situation in the past did not continue afterwards and another situation has occurred. It indicates that the past situation has finished. It is attached to an adjective or a verb. –았었– is used when the last vowel in the adjective stem is ㅏ or ㅗ. For all other vowel endings of the adjective or verb stem, –었었– is used.

Basic form	–았/었었–	Basic form	–았/었었–
크다	컸었어요	살다	살았었어요
작다	작았었어요	듣다	들었었어요
길다	길었었어요	돕다	도왔었어요
덥다	더웠었어요	짓다	지었었어요
가다	갔었어요	학생이다	학생이었었어요
먹다	먹었었어요	친구이다	친구였었어요

ex A: 고등학교 때도 지금처럼 날씬했어요?
B: 아니요. 고등학교 때는 좀 뚱뚱했었어요.

ex A: 작년 여름휴가 때 어디에 갔었어요?
B: 부산에 갔었어요.

ex A: 유키 씨를 알아요?
B: 네. 지난 학기에 같은 반 친구였었어요.

Focus Plus

- –았/었– is used when something occurred in the past but its consequence still remains or continues to influence the present.

ex A: 이치로 씨, 나타샤 씨한테서 전화 왔어요. 전화 받으세요.
B: 네. 고마워요.

ex A: 이치로 씨, 나타샤 씨한테서 전화 왔었어요.
B: 아 그래요? 언제요?
A: 1시간쯤 전에요.

Answers

① A: 장소이 씨는 한국어를 할 줄 알아요?
B: 네. 5년 전에는 한국어를 전혀 못했었는데 지금은 한국어를 할 줄 알아요.

② A: 이치로 씨는 회사원이에요?
B: 네. 5년 전에는 대학교에 다녔었는데 지금은 회사원이에요.

③ A: 왕카이 씨는 키가 커요?
B: 네. 5년 전에는 키가 작았었는데 지금은 키가 커요.

④ A: 한준영 씨는 해외 출장을 자주 다녀요?
B: 네. 5년 전에는 출장이 거의 없었었는데 지금은 해외 출장을 자주 다녀요.

⑤ A: 티엔 씨는 성격이 활발해요?
B: 네. 5년 전에는 성격이 내성적이었었는데 지금은 성격이 활발해요.

Grammar Focus

–았/었던 is used when the speaker is reminded again of something that already happened in the past and has now ended after the speaker saw or experienced it. It indicates that what happened in the past has been cut off or interrupted and is not connected to the present. It is attached to an adjective or a verb. It modifies a noun in conjunction with an adjective or verb. –았던 is used when the last vowel in the adjective stem is ㅏ or ㅗ. For all other vowel endings of the adjective or verb stem, –었던 is used.

Basic form	–았/었던	Basic form	–았/었던	Basic form	–았/었던
예쁘다	예뻤던	가다	갔던	듣다	들었던
작다	작았던	먹다	먹었던	돕다	도왔던
덥다	더웠던	살다	살았던	짓다	지었던

ex A: 어제 동창회에서 만난 친구들은 어땠어요?
B: 오랜만에 만나서 반가웠어요. 그런데 초등학교 때는 키가 작았던 친구가 지금은 키가 커서 깜짝 놀랐어요.

ex A: 아내를 처음 만났을 때 어땠어요?
B: 정말 좋았어요. 그날 정말 아름다웠던 제 아내는 마치 장미꽃 같았어요.

ex A: 어제 누구 만났어요?
B: 중학교 때 같이 공부했던 친구를 만났어요.

ex A: 유키 씨 결혼식에 무슨 옷을 입을 거예요?
B: 지난번 친구 결혼식 때 입었던 원피스를 입을까 해요.

Focus Plus

- –았/었던 것 같다 is used when you reminisce over a past experience and make a guess about the situation at the time. It is mostly used when the speaker's memory is not so accurate.

ex A: 영민 씨는 지난 번 모임에 왔나요?
B: 글쎄요. 안 왔던 것 같아요.

Answers

① 어젯밤에 꾸었던 꿈을 무서워서 잊을 수가 없습니다.
② 신혼여행 때 묵었던 호텔에 5년 후에 다시 가기로 했습니다.
③ 초등학교 때 좋아했던 친구를 어제 길에서 보았습니다.
④ 언니가 결혼할 때 입었던 웨딩드레스를 내가 다시 입기로 했습니다.
⑤ 작년에 비행기 안에서 만났던 아주머니를 집 근처에서 우연히 만났습니다.

 p.148

Grammar Focus

반말 is used when talking to close friends or people younger than you. In this intimate, casual way of speaking the declarative endings –습니다, –아/어요 become –아/어, the interrogative endings –습니까, –아/어요? become –아/어, the propositive endings –(으)십시오, –(으)세요 become –아/어, and the imperative endings –(으)십시오, –(으)세요 become –아/어. When you call someone's name, you can say name+아/야. When giving answers, 네 and 아니요 become 응 and 아니 respectively.

declarative form(–습니다, –아/어요)

Basic form	–아/어	–았/었어	–(으)ㄹ 거야
가다	가	갔어	갈 거야
읽다	읽어	읽었어	읽을 거야

exhortative form(–(으)ㅂ시다, –아/어요)

Basic form	–자	–지 말자
가다	가자	가지 말자
읽다	읽자	읽지 말자

interrogative form(–습니까?, –아/어요?)

Basic form	–아/어	–았/었어	–(으)ㄹ 거야
가다	가?	갔어?	갈 거야?
읽다	읽어?	읽었어?	읽을 거야?

imperative form(–(으)십시오, –(으)세요)

Basic form	–아/어	–지 마
가다	가	가지 마
읽다	읽어	읽지 마

Names and answers

Name	–아/야	Answer	응/아니
수진	수진아	네	응
철수	철수야	아니요	아니

ex A: 오랜만이야. 어떻게 지냈어?
B: 잘 지냈어.

ex A: 요코야, 이번 주말에 약속 있어?
B: 아니, 약속 없어.

ex A: 늦어서 미안해.
B: 괜찮아. 그런데 무슨 일 있었어?

Answers

① A: 언니, 삼계탕은 뭐로 만들어요?
B: 삼계탕은 닭고기로 만들어.

② A: 너는 어떤 케이크를 좋아해?
B: 난 케이크를 안 좋아해.

③ A: 선배, 이 샌드위치 먹어도 돼요?
B: 안 돼. 오래됐으니까 먹지 마.

④ A: 오빠, 엄마 생신에 무엇을 선물할까?
B: 꽃바구니를 선물하자.

p.149

Vocabulary & Expression

그때 보자

그때 보자 means *see you then*. It is a promise to meet at an agreed time. You can also say 그날 보자, and use honorific sentences such as 그때 뵙겠습니다 or 그날 뵙겠습니다.

ex A: 이번 동창회 모임에 올 거지?
B: 응, 그때 보자.

ex A: 토요일 한 시에 만나자. 그날 다시 연락 줄게.
B: 응, 그래. 그럼 그날 보자.

ex A: 다음 주에 하는 송년회 모임에 오시지요?
B: 네. 그때 뵙겠습니다.

ex A: 이번 학기 신입생 환영회에 가십니까?
B: 네. 그날 뵙겠습니다.

Script

There is one new voice mail.

Hi, Sally? How have you been? It's me, Yulia. Since you didn't answer the phone, I'm leaving a voice mail. Well, the reason I called is that we decided to get together with our friends who studied together at Ewha Womans University.
You remember Shinji and Rie, don't you? We studied together in level 1. They're getting married next month. So we'd like to congratulate them and besides, James is in Korea. He hasn''t been here in a long time.
We're going to meet at 4 p.m. on Saturday the 13th, at the school front gate. When we get together, we're going to say hello to the teacher who taught us. A lot of people are coming; you should come too. At 4 o'clock Saturday on January 13, okay? I'll send you a text message as well.
See you then.

Answers

(1) ③
They are getting together to congratulate their friends' wedding and to meet a friend who came to Korea for the first time in a long time.

(2) ①, ④, ⑤

(3) ①
Yulia and her classmates are supposed to meet at 4 o'clock on Saturday the 13th at the school front gate. So the text message Yulia sent is ①.

Vocabulary & Expression

우리가 마지막으로 본 게 언제였지?

우리가 마지막으로 본 게 언제였지? means ***when was the last time we saw each other?*** It is an expression used to start a conversation with someone you haven't seen for a while, asking when the last time you met was and reminiscing about the old days.

ex A: 우리가 마지막으로 본 게 언제였지?
B: 작년 8월이었어. 그때 네 생일이었어.
A: 맞아. 그 때 네가 나에게 책을 선물해 줬었잖아. 정말 좋았어.
B: 응. 네가 좋아할 줄 알고 준비했었지.

Functional Expression

- **Speaking fondly of old memories**

  When you look back on old memories and reminisce about the good old days, you can use expressions such as 그때가 그리워, 그때가 정말 좋았어, 그때로 돌아가고 싶어, 그때가 생각나, etc.

  ex A: 우리가 한국에서 같이 공부하던 때 기억나?
  B: 그럼 그때 정말 재미있었는데. 그때가 그리워. /
  그때 기억은 잊을 수 없어. 그때가 정말 좋았어. /
  그때 기억이 생생해. 다시 그때로 돌아가고 싶어. /
  응, 그때 정말 좋았었는데. 아직도 그때가 생각나.

Dialogue

Yulia	Sally, it's been a long time. How have you been?
Sally	Fine. So great to see you.
Yulia	When was the last time we saw each other?
Sally	Probably last year, at graduation.
Yulia	You're right. I was so sorry to say goodbye to my friends that day. We were all very close.
Sally	Yes, we were. Do you remember when we went to see the traditional drum concert with the culture class? When the show ended, we all went up on stage and learned how to play the drum, didn't we?
Yulia	Yes, I remember. Then, you got lost in the folk village. So we had to make an announcement to find you. The teacher was really worried then.
Sally	That's right. I really panicked too.
Yulia	The teacher we went to the folk village with was Ms. Cho Sumi, right?
Sally	Yes, she was such a fun teacher. Her voice was very loud during class too.
Yulia	Wow, I still remember everything clearly.
Sally	Yes. I really miss that time.

Grammar Focus

–아/어지다 is used to indicate that a certain thing is gradually changing into a different state. It is attached to an adjective, and –아지다 is used if the last vowel of the adjective stem is ㅏ or ㅗ, and –어지다 is used with all the other vowels.

Basic form	–아/어지다	Basic form	–아/어지다
크다	커지다	복잡하다	복잡해지다
예쁘다	예뻐지다	넓다	넓어지다
나쁘다	나빠지다	멀다	멀어지다
작다	작아지다	춥다	추워지다
좋다	좋아지다	빨갛다	빨개지다

ex A: 어제 고등학교 동창회에 갔었지요? 어땠어요?
B: 친구들을 오랜만에 만나서 좋았어요. 그리고 친구들이 고등학교 때보다 더 예뻐졌어요.

ex A: 미셸 씨 옷이 왜 그래요?
B: 집에서 물빨래했는데 옷이 이렇게 작아졌어요.

ex A: 오랜만에 고향에 왔더니 변한 것이 많네요.
B: 네, 맞아요. 건물도 많아지고 거리도 복잡해졌어요.

ex A: 날씨가 꽤 추워졌네요.
B: 네. 환절기라서 쌀쌀해졌어요. 감기 조심하세요.

ex A: 아직 5월인데 날씨가 더운 것 같아요.
B: 네, 그런데 6월이 되면 더 더워질 거예요.

ex A: 여자 친구와는 자주 연락해요?
B: 아니요. 저는 공부 때문에, 여자 친구는 회사 일 때문에 서로 연락을 자주 못해요. 그래서 요즘 사이가 멀어지는 것 같아요.

ex A: 이치로 씨, 왜 이렇게 얼굴이 빨개졌어요?
B: 저는 말하기 발표만 하면 얼굴이 빨개져요.

Answers

① 나무가 10년 전에 비해서 적어졌습니다.
② 공기가 10년 전에 비해서 나빠졌습니다.
③ 길이 10년 전에 비해서 넓어졌습니다.
④ 사람이 10년 전에 비해서 많아졌습니다.

 p.153

Grammar Focus

낮춤말 is used when a superior or older person talks to people who are lower in rank or younger in age. In 낮춤말, the lowest level of speech, the declarative endings –습니다, –아/어요 become –아/어 or –ㄴ/는다, the interrogative endings –습니까?, –아/어요? become –니?, the propositive endings –(으)ㅂ시다, –아/어요 become –자, and the imperative endings –(으)십시오, –(으)세요 become –아/어라.

declarative form(–습니다, –아/어요)

Basic form	–아/어	–았/었어	–(으)ㄹ 거야
보다	봐	봤어	볼 거야
입다	입어	입었어	입을 거야

exhortative form(–(으)ㅂ시다, –아/어요)

Basic form	–자	–지 말자
보다	보자	보지 말자
입다	입자	입지 말자

interrogative form(–습니까?, –아/어요?)

Basic form	–아/어	–았/었어	–(으)ㄹ 거야
보다	보니?	봤니?	볼 거니?
입다	입니?	입었니?	입을 거니?

imperative form(–(으)십시오, –(으)세요)

Basic form	–아/어	–지 마
보다	봐라	보지 마라
입다	입어라	입지 마라

ex A: 선배, 주말에 뭐 했어요?
B: 이번에 새로 나온 영화 봤어.

ex A: (어머니가 아들에게) 저녁은 먹었니?
B: 네, 친구하고 먹었어요.

Focus Plus

- The lowest level of speech and casual level of speech: the endings are the same in declarative and propositive sentences but different in interrogative and imperative sentences.

Basic form	familiar speech interrogative form			familiar speech imperative form	
	–아/어니	았/었니	(으)ㄹ 거니	–아/어라	–지 마라
보다	보니?	봤니?	볼 거니?	봐라	보지 마라
입다	입니?	입었니?	입을 거니?	입어라	입지 마라

Basic form	intimate speech interrogative form			intimate speech imperative form	
	–아/어	았/었어	(으)ㄹ 거야	–아/어	–지 마
보다	봐?	봤어?	볼 거야?	봐	보지 마
입다	입어?	입었어?	입을 거야?	입어	입지 마

Answers

민호야,
엄마는 할인 마트에 장 보러 갔다가 올 거야.
식탁 위에 있는 간식을 ① 먹어라. 텔레비전을 너무 오래 ② 보지 마라.
알겠지? 오늘도 승민이 집에 ③ 놀러 갈 거니? 밖에 나갈 거면 6시까지
④ 돌아와라. 저녁에 엄마하고 같이 피아노를 ⑤ 연습하자.

엄마가

Vocabulary & Expression

엊그제 같다

엊그제 같다 means ***it seems like it was yesterday***. It indicates that it feels like not so much time has passed. **엊그제** is short for **어제 그제** meaning 'just a few days ago.'

ex A: 한국에 있는 동안 고마웠어요. 저 내일 일본에 가요.
B: 한국에 온 게 엊그제 같은데 벌써 고향에 갈 때가 됐구나.

그렇게 말해 줘서 고맙구나

그렇게 말해 줘서 고맙구나 means ***thanks for saying that***. It is a response to something nice the other person has said. **고맙구나** is a casual form of **고맙군요**.

ex A: 선생님, 한국어 공부를 많이 도와주셔서 정말 고맙습니다. 한국어를 잘하게 된 건 모두 선생님 덕분이에요.
B: 그렇게 말해 줘서 고맙구나.

그럴게요

그럴게요 means ***I will***. It shows the speaker's intent to do what the other person says. It can be replaced with **그렇게 할게요**.

ex A: 일본에 돌아가면 꼭 연락 주세요.
B: 네, <u>그럴게요</u>.(= 그렇게 할게요)

뵈러 올게요

뵈러 올게요 means ***I'll come to see (you)***. It is used when speaking with one's elders or superiors and means that the speaker will come to see the elder person or superior. **뵈다** is an honorific form of 'meet' or 'see.'

ex A: 많이 보고 싶을 거예요.
B: 저도요. 한국에 오면 꼭 선생님 뵈러 또 올게요.

Functional Expression

- **Saying you have come to make a greeting**

  To say that the purpose of your visit is to make a greeting, expressions such as 뵈러 왔어요, 인사드리러 왔어요 and 인사드리려고 왔습니다 can be used. 뵈다 and 인사드리다 are honorific forms of speech.

  ex A: 어떻게 오셨어요?
  B: 교장 선생님 좀 뵈러 왔어요. /
  교장 선생님 좀 뵈려고 왔는데요. /
  교장 선생님께 인사드리러 왔어요. /
  교장 선생님께 인사드리려고 왔습니다.

- **Saying that you think time has gone fast**

  To say that time flew by, expressions such as 시간이 참 빨리 가다, 시간이 정말 빠르다, or 처음 본 게 엊그제 같다 can be used.

  ex A: 저, 공부가 다 끝나서 내일 고향으로 돌아가요.
  B: 벌써요? 시간이 정말 빠르군요. / 벌써요? 시간이 참 빨리 가네요. /
  처음 본 게 엊그제 같은데 벌써 돌아갈 날이 되었군요. /
  그래요? 처음 본 게 엊그제 같은데 벌써 돌아가는군요.

Script

Restaurant owner	Come in.
Zhang Souyi	Grandma, how are you?
Restaurant owner	Hello, It's been a while. What can I get you?
Zhang Souyi	I just came to say goodbye today. I am going back to China since I've finished my studies.
Restaurant owner	Already? It feels like yesterday that you first came here. Time really flies. Has it been a year already?
Zhang Souyi	Yes. I was just getting used to life in Korea and started to enjoy it a lot. I can't believe I have to leave now.
Restaurant owner	Me neither. You came to our restaurant often and it was fun to hear you talk about this and that and to drink the tea you brought from China. You were like my granddaughter.
Zhang Souyi	You always made such delicious food. I don't think I'll forget it even when I go back to China.
Restaurant owner	Thanks for saying that. Study hard in China. And if you ever come to Korea again, make sure you stop by.
Zhang Souyi	Yes, I will. Grandma, I don't have any photos of us together. Let's take one now.
Restaurant owner	Sure, let's do it.
Zhang Souyi	Grandma, stay healthy. If I come to Korea, I'll come and visit you.
Restaurant owner	Yes, thank you. Bye bye.

Answers

(1) ①

(2) ② Since Zhang Souyi did not have a picture of her and Grandma together, she took a picture today.

(3) ① 아니요 ② 아니요 ③ 네

Zhang Souyi has finished her studies and goes back to China tomorrow. The restaurant lady said that it had already been a year since she met Zhang Souyi. 'Already a year' suggests that time has passed faster than expected. The restaurant lady said that she liked Zhang Souyi a lot because she was like a granddaughter to her.

오랜만에 만난 선배에게 안부 묻기

p.156

Vocabulary & Expression

연락이 끊겨서 소식이 궁금했어요

연락이 끊겨서 소식이 궁금했어요 means ***that (I) lost contact with (them), so (I) was wondering how (they) were doing.*** This expression indicates that the speaker lost contact with someone/some people and was wondering how they were doing. 연락이 끊기다 indicates loss of contact between people who once stayed in touch. Expressions such as 소식이 끊기다, 연락이 끊기다 can be used.

ex A: 동아리 선배들은 어떻게 지내요? 선배들과 연락이 끊겨서 소식이 궁금해요.
B: 모두 정신없이 바쁘게 지내고 있어.

ex A: 지난 학기에 함께 공부했던 티엔 씨와 연락해요?
B: 아니요. 학기가 끝난 후에 연락이 끊겼어요.

ex A: 가오리 씨는 잘 지내요?
B: 아니요. 가오리 씨와 소식이 끊긴 지 1년이 넘었어요.

정신이 없어요

정신이 없어요 means ***things are very hectic.*** It indicates that one is very busy. 정신이 없다 means that one is very busy and is used to emphasize the fact. It can be replaced with 정신없이 바쁘다.

ex A: 요즘 많이 바빠요?
B: 네. 요즘 발표 준비 때문에 정신이 없어요. (= 정신없이 바빠요)

안부 전해 주세요

안부 전해 주세요 means ***please tell him/her I said hello.*** It is used to ask someone to pass on words of greeting to someone else. 안부 indicates news of a person's welfare, or the act of asking how another person is doing.

ex A: 선생님, 오랜만이에요. 잘 지내셨어요?
B: 네. 이치로 씨도 잘 지냈지요? 지난 학기 우리 반 친구들이 보고 싶네요. 모두에게 안부 전해 주세요.

ex A: 오랜만이다. 잘 지냈어? 우리 엄마가 네 안부 자주 물으셨는데.
B: 그래? 나는 잘 지냈어. 어머니께 안부 전해 드려 줘.

Functional Expression

- **Encouraging someone in casual speech**

When encouraging your friends or someone younger than you at school or at home who is having a hard time, you can use a casual level of speech.

ex A: 힘내. / 기운 내. / 행운을 빌어. / 행운을 빈다. /
다 잘 될 거야. / 용기를 잃지 마. / 좋은 일이 있을 거야.
B: 응, 고마워, 형.

- **Thanking in casual speech**

When thanking a *seonbae* (senior at school, work etc.) for encouraging comments you can use a casual level of speech. When a *seonbae* who is close to you says something that makes you feel good you can thank him or her in a casual speech.

ex A: 가장 중요한 건 한국어 실력이야. 지금부터 열심히 공부하면 다 잘 될 거야. 힘내.
B: 선배 말이 힘이 되었어. /
조언해 줘서 정말 고마워. /
선배 덕분에 걱정이 줄었어. /
선배 말을 듣고 나니까 힘이 나. /
선배 조언이 많은 도움이 되었어.

Dialogue

Tien	*Seonbae*, long time no see.
Gaorii	It's been a while. How have you been doing? Have you gotten used to life at school?
Tien	Yes. But I've been busy getting ready for college admissions. How about you?
Gaorii	I've been doing fine. I'm going to Japan for a while this vacation. Rie is getting married.
Tien	Really? Rie is getting married? What about the other *seonbaes* from our club, how are they doing?
Gaorii	They went back to the States and graduated from university, or came back to Korea and are attending graduate school here. Anna got a job at a Korean travel agency. Everybody is frantically busy.
Tien	I lost contact with them, so I was wondering how they were doing. Do you know their email addresses or phone numbers by any chance?
Gaorii	Yes, I do. Yulia's phone number is 010-2323-3562 and Anna's is 010-3987-1267. By the way, how is your preparation for college admission going?
Tien	I'm so stressed out because of that. What is most important?
Gaorii	The most important thing is your language skills in Korean, so study hard now. If you want to take classes and do homework at university, you cannot get by with bad Korean skills.
Tien	Nothing easy about it. Thanks for your advice. Send my regards to Rie *seonbae*.
Gaorii	Alright. Good luck. Let's stay in touch.

Vocabulary & Expression

그리워질 때

그리워질 때 means ***when one misses someone/something***. 그립다 means to have a great longing to see someone or something and is used in expressions such as 고향이 그립다, 가족이 그립다 etc.

ex A: 가족이 그리워질 때 어떻게 해요?
B: 가족과 전화 통화하거나 가족사진을 찾아 봐요.

ex A: 티엔 씨, 저 요즘 고향 음식이 너무 그리워요.
B: 그럼 우리 이번 주말에 베트남 식당에 가서 고향 음식을 먹을까요?

몸살

몸살 means ***a fever with aches and pains***. When your body is very tired, you might get an illness called 몸살, the symptoms of which are body aches, bodily weakness, and fever. When you have these symptoms, you can say 몸살(이) 나다.

ex A: 얼굴이 안 좋아요. 무슨 일 있어요?
B: 요즘 시험 준비로 며칠 잠을 못 자서 몸살이 났어요.

ex A: 명절 잘 보냈어요?
B: 네, 그런데 몸살이 난 것 같아요.

Functional Expression

- **Writing an opening greeting on a letter or email**

Letters and emails start with a greeting of some kind. This greeting may be an inquiry into the receiver's welfare or a comment about the weather.

ex 안녕하세요? 잘 지내세요? /
안녕하세요? 어떻게 지내세요? /
안녕하십니까? 건강은 어떠십니까? /
쌀쌀한 날씨에 안녕하신지요? /
안녕하세요? 요즘 날씨가 꽤 추워졌네요. /
안녕하십니까? 요즘 환절기라서 일교차가 크네요. /
안녕하세요? 단풍이 참 아름다운 계절입니다. /
안녕하세요? 더운 여름이 가고 가을을 맞이하는 9월입니다

Pronunciation

Euphony/ Lateralization

ㄴ is pronounced as [ㄹ] when it comes after the final consonant ㄹ. Additionally, the final consonant ㄴ is usually pronounced as [ㄹ] when it comes before ㄹ. This change in pronunciation is called 'euphony' or 'lateralization'.

ex 몸살 나서[몸살라서], 생일날[생일랄], 물냉면[물랭면], 일 년[일련] 연락[열락]

Text

Dear boarding house lady,

How are you? This is Zhang Souyi. I lived in room 102 until December last year. I hope you are doing well. I am writing this letter because I was wondering how you were and also because I have a favor to ask you.

I am now back in China and got a job at the company I have always wanted to work for. It is a trading company and since we have business with Korea, we use the Korean language a lot. Life here is very busy and hectic.

But there are times when I miss life in Korea. You were so nice to us, so I did not feel lonely and everyone there was very kind. So I really enjoyed studying in Korea. Especially when I got sick and was suffering from aches and pains, the food you cooked was really delicious. The seaweed soup that you made on my birthday, the rice cake soup we had on New Year's Day, and the cold noodles you made on a really hot day—I still think of them. I was not lonely the whole year thanks to you. I really appreciate it.

I'm sorry but I need to ask you a favor. Is there any mail for me? A friend of mine is returning to China and she promised to bring all my mail if there is any at the boarding house. When she stops by, can you please give my mail to her? Thank you.

Please take care of your health and if you visit Beijing, please let me know. I will give you a tour.

Best regards,
Zhang Souyi
January 30

Answers

(1) ③

Zhang Souyi wrote a letter to find out how the boarding house lady is doing and to ask her to pass on any mail to her friend. She is not writing to ask for Korean food. But she did say she thinks about the food that the boarding house lady cooked for her.

(2) ① 아니요　② 네　③ 아니요

Zhang Souyi got a job when she went back to China. So she was employed in a company in China, not in Korea. Also, it is not known that the boarding house lady has a plan to visit China.

(3) ① 아팠을 때 병원에 같이 가 주셨습니다. ② 맛있는 음식을 해 주셨습니다.

Vocabulary Check

▶ **Tick off the words and expressions that you know.**

소식과 안부	News and Regards
☐ 새로운 소식을 듣다	to hear fresh news
☐ 소식을 기다리다	to await news (from someone)
☐ 소식을 알다	to know the news
☐ 소식이 끊기다	to lose touch (with someone)
☐ 소식이 빠르다	to be quick to hear the news
☐ 소식이 없다	to not know the news
☐ 소식이 오다	to hear from someone
☐ 안부가 궁금하다	to ask how someone is doing
☐ 안부를 묻다	to say hello
☐ 안부를 전하다	to send one's regards to someone
☐ 안부 문자를 보내다	to send one's regards in a text message
☐ 안부 인사를 드리다	to send one's regards
☐ 안부 전화를 하다	to call someone as a greeting
☐ 안부 편지를 쓰다	to write a letter as a greeting
☐ 연락이 끊기다	to lose contact

인사 방법	Methods of Greeting
☐ 고개를 숙이다	to bow
☐ 목례하다	to nod
☐ 볼에 입을 맞추다	to kiss the cheek
☐ 손을 흔들다	to wave one's hand
☐ 악수를 하다	to shake hands
☐ 인사를 받다	to receive a greeting
☐ 절을 하다	to bow
☐ 팔을 벌리다	to open one's arms
☐ 포옹하다	to hug
☐ 허리를 굽혀서 인사하다	to bow low

인사	Greeting
☐ 감사 인사를 드리다	to thank someone
☐ 눈인사를 하다	to greet with the eyes
☐ 새해 인사를 드리다	to make a New Year's greeting
☐ 작별 인사를 나누다	to say goodbye
☐ 첫 인사를 나누다	to greet someone for the first time
☐ 축하 인사를 하다	to congratulate someone
☐ 환영 인사를 하다	to welcome someone

추억	Memories
☐ 그립다	to miss/long for someone/something
☐ 기쁘다	to be happy
☐ 기억에 남다	to remain in one's memory
☐ 기억이 생생하다	to remember vividly
☐ 반갑다	to be pleased
☐ 섭섭하다	to feel sad
☐ 아쉽다	to regret
☐ 잊지 못할 기억이다	to be an unforgettable memory
☐ 작별하다	to part
☐ 추억이 되다	to become a memory
☐ 헤어지다	to break up

Glossary

Ⓣ Textbook Ⓢ Study Guide

1등석에 앉다 to fly first class Ⓣ 130 Ⓢ 107

1인1실 single room Ⓣ 119, 121 Ⓢ 93

2인1실 twin room Ⓣ 119 Ⓢ 93

3단 우산 3-fold umbrella Ⓣ 31

가난하다 to be poor Ⓣ 89, 161

가능하다 to be available Ⓣ 111, 149, 167 Ⓢ 15, 90, 96, 98

가득 fully Ⓣ 89

가루비누 soap powder Ⓣ 84, 85, 88, 111 Ⓢ 65, 81

가리키다 to point to Ⓣ 68, 69 Ⓢ 49

가방을 들다 to hold a bag Ⓢ 10, 23

가보로 남기다 to hand down as a family treasure Ⓣ 89

가속이 붙다 to catch speed Ⓣ 107

가요 Korean popular songs Ⓣ 65

가족들이 모이다 to have the family gather together Ⓣ 47, 165 Ⓢ 37

가죽 leather Ⓣ 30, 31 Ⓢ 20

가지각색 all kinds Ⓣ 35

각각 each Ⓣ 35, 106, 160

간단하다 to be simple Ⓣ 33, 74, 82, 110, 120, 121, 123, 141 Ⓢ 59, 80, 90

간섭받다 to be intruded Ⓣ 114, 115 Ⓢ 85, 93

간섭하다 to intrude Ⓣ 114, 115 Ⓢ 93

간식 snack Ⓣ 153 Ⓢ 114

갈색 brown Ⓣ 28, 31, 164 Ⓢ 13, 23

갈아입다 to change clothes Ⓣ 137, 168

갈아타다 to transfer Ⓣ 102, 103, 104 Ⓢ 77, 82

감사 인사를 드리다 to thank someone Ⓢ 121

감사장을 쓰다 to write a thank-you card Ⓣ 76 Ⓢ 65

값지다 to be valuable Ⓣ 89

강남 south of the river Ⓣ 122, 123, 168 Ⓢ 92

강북 north of the river Ⓣ 122, 123, 168 Ⓢ 92

강아지 puppy Ⓣ 29, 164 Ⓢ 18, 20

같다 to be the same Ⓣ 25, 27, 32, 33, 40, 43, 50, 51, 57, 68, 70, 74, 75, 78, 82, 84, 85, 88, 89, 110, 111, 117, 120, 121, 140, 164, 166 Ⓢ 80, 93, 108

같은 방 친구 roommate Ⓣ 57, 110, 111, 120, 121 Ⓢ 80, 93

개강 beginning of semester Ⓣ 86, 87, 95 Ⓢ 63

개인 individual Ⓣ 115 Ⓢ 93

개인 샤워실이 있다 to have a private shower booth Ⓣ 115 Ⓢ 93

개조하다 to renovate Ⓣ 104

걱정이 줄다 to have less worries Ⓣ 157, 166 Ⓢ 118

건물 building Ⓣ 152 Ⓢ 39, 113

검색 search Ⓣ 65, 165 Ⓢ 46, 51

검토하다 to review Ⓣ 82 Ⓢ 59

겉 outside Ⓣ 89

결과 result, outcome, consequence Ⓣ 69, 116, 117 Ⓢ 96

결석하다 to be absent Ⓣ 110 Ⓢ 60, 80

결혼기념일 wedding anniversary Ⓣ Ⓢ 37

결혼식 wedding Ⓣ 40, 44, 89, 149 Ⓢ 18, 29, 37, 43, 60, 109

결혼식장 wedding hall Ⓣ 149

결혼하다 to marry Ⓣ 45, 156, 157 Ⓢ 65

경부고속도로 Gyeongbu Expressway Ⓣ 101, 167 Ⓢ 79

경비실 doorman's office Ⓣ 119 Ⓢ 93

경쟁률 competition ratio Ⓢ105

무게 weight Ⓣ 59, 60 Ⓢ 42, 51
무게를 달다 to weigh Ⓣ 59 Ⓢ 51
무대 stage Ⓣ 150, 151
묵을 곳을 찾다 to look for somewhere to lodge Ⓢ 79
문자 메시지 text message Ⓣ 149 Ⓢ 43
물건 object Ⓣ 30, 31, 41, 88, 96, 97, 112, 122, 134, 139, 142, 164 Ⓢ 20, 27, 37, 82, 93, 96, 98, 99, 107
물건을 사기 편하다 to be convenient for shopping Ⓣ 122 Ⓢ 93
물건을 사다 to buy a product Ⓣ 134 Ⓢ 107
물건을 착각하다 to mistake an object for something else Ⓢ 107
뮤지컬 musical Ⓣ 62 Ⓢ 43
미끄럽다 to be slippery Ⓣ 99
미니스커트 miniskirt Ⓢ 23
미리 예약하다 to book in advance Ⓣ 135, 142, 166 Ⓢ 100, 106
미만 less than Ⓣ 86
미아 lost child Ⓣ 29 Ⓢ 18
미역국 seaweed soup Ⓣ 158, 159
미용실 hair salon Ⓣ 21 Ⓢ 25
민소매 티셔츠 sleeveless shirt Ⓢ 23
민속촌 Folk Village Ⓣ 150, 151

바뀌다 to be changed Ⓣ 74, 94, 98, 100 Ⓢ 72, 79
바로 right away Ⓣ 24, 25, 30, 31, 56, 58, 66, 67, 94 Ⓢ 19, 44, 48, 60, 68
박씨 gourd seed Ⓣ 161
반갑다 to be pleased Ⓣ 120, 150 Ⓢ 121
반납하다 to return Ⓣ 63 Ⓢ 44, 51, 54
반대하다 to oppose Ⓣ 84, 85, 116 Ⓢ 86
반바지 shorts Ⓣ 42, 43, 77 Ⓢ 10, 23
반바지를 입다 to wear shorts Ⓣ 42, 43, 77 Ⓢ 10, 23
반지를 끼다 to wear a ring Ⓢ 23
반짝이다 to shine Ⓢ 18
반팔 티셔츠 short-sleeved T-shirt Ⓢ 23
발급 issue Ⓣ 66, 67 Ⓢ 40, 47, 51
발급되다 to be issued Ⓣ 67 Ⓢ 40, 47
발음 pronunciation Ⓣ 22, 33, 51, 69 Ⓢ 12, 21
밤색 chestnut brown Ⓣ 28 Ⓢ 23
밥그릇 rice bowl Ⓣ 77, 166
방값을 물어보다 to ask the price of a room Ⓢ 93
방금 just now Ⓣ 82 Ⓢ 24, 46, 59
방문 room door Ⓣ 68, 69 Ⓢ 88
방문하다 to visit Ⓣ 76, 77, 96, 97 Ⓢ 65
방송 (broadcast) announcement Ⓣ 29, 75, 101, 139, 150, 151, 164, 167 Ⓢ 18, 19, 74
방송실 broadcasting room Ⓣ 164
방울 bell Ⓣ 164
방해가 되다 to be bothering Ⓣ 167 Ⓢ 88
배가 고프다 to be hungry Ⓣ 80, 110 Ⓢ 57, 86
배낭여행 backpacking trip Ⓣ 104, 105
배낭을 메다 to put on/wear a backpack Ⓢ 10, 23
배달 소요 시간을 묻다 to ask how long delivery will take Ⓢ 51
배달 요금을 내다 to pay the postage fee Ⓢ 51
배달시키다 to order delivery Ⓣ 82
배터리 battery Ⓣ 102, 103 Ⓢ 75
배편으로 보내다 to send by surface mail Ⓣ 59, 61 Ⓢ 42, 43, 51

빠른 길로 가다 to go the fast way Ⓣ 96 Ⓢ 79

빠른 길을 알려주다 to inform someone of a shortcut Ⓣ 96 Ⓢ 79

빠른우편으로 보내다 to send by express mail Ⓣ 59, 61 Ⓢ 51

빨간색 red Ⓣ 28, 29, 40, 98, 106, 164 Ⓢ 17, 23, 26, 72

빨갛다 to be red Ⓣ 27, 34 Ⓢ 17, 113

빼앗기다 to be robbed of Ⓣ 161

사 오다 to buy Ⓣ 53

사거리 crossroad Ⓣ 92, 96, 97 Ⓢ 71, 79

사생활 one's private life Ⓣ 114, 115 Ⓢ 85, 93

사생활을 간섭 받다 to have one's private life intruded upon Ⓣ 115 Ⓢ 85

사생활을 간섭하다 to intrude on someone's private life Ⓣ 93

사업을 시작하다 to start one's own business Ⓣ 65

사업이 잘되다 to do well in business Ⓣ 75, 99 Ⓢ 53

사전을 찾다 to look up the dictionary Ⓣ 64 Ⓢ 45

산골 deep in the mountains Ⓣ 143

살구 apricot Ⓣ 143

삶 life Ⓣ 35 Ⓢ 52

삼거리 three-way junction Ⓢ 79

삼계탕 ginseng chicken soup Ⓣ 148 Ⓢ 110

상관없다 to be irrelevant Ⓣ 32

상급생 senior student Ⓣ 35

상다리가 부러지다 table to be loaded with food Ⓢ 61

상영 시간 running time Ⓣ 140, 141 Ⓢ 107

상영 시간이 되다 to be the start of screening time Ⓢ 107

상의하다 to discuss Ⓣ 84, 85, 166 Ⓢ 62, 65

새 집으로 이사를 하다 to move to a new house Ⓢ 65

새로 newly 53, 66, 67, 75, 86, 99, 111, 113, 120, 121, 139 Ⓢ 11, 46, 47, 53, 73, 75, 81, 87, 93, 114

새로 이사할 곳을 알아보다 to look for a place to move to Ⓢ 93

새로운 소식을 듣다 to hear fresh news Ⓢ 121

새벽 dawn Ⓣ 68, 69

새해 인사를 드리다 to make a New Year's greeting Ⓢ 121

새해 인사를 하다 to make New Year's greetings Ⓢ 37

샌들 sandals Ⓣ 77 Ⓢ 23, 54

생기다 to come into existence, occur Ⓣ 24, 117, 123, 131, 168 Ⓢ 96, 107

생김생김(=생김새) looks Ⓣ 35

생생하다 to be vivid Ⓣ 150, 151 Ⓢ 112, 121

생활용품 daily supplies Ⓣ 84, 85, 88 Ⓢ 62, 65

샤워실 shower room Ⓣ 115, 119 Ⓢ 93

서두르다 to hurry Ⓣ 138, 139 Ⓢ 104

서명 signature Ⓣ 62, 66, 67 Ⓢ 51

서명(책의 이름) book title Ⓣ 65, 165

서명을 하다 to sign one's name Ⓣ 62, 66, 67 Ⓢ 51

서비스로 받다 to receive for free Ⓢ 107

서울역 Seoul Station Ⓣ 93, 96, 97 Ⓢ 67

서지다 to stop against one's will Ⓣ 125

선글라스 sunglasses Ⓣ 43 Ⓢ 23

선물을 교환하다 to exchange gifts Ⓢ 37

선물을 상의하다 to ask one's advice about a gift Ⓢ 65

선비 scholar Ⓣ 89

섭섭하다 to feel sad Ⓣ 150, 151 Ⓢ 121

예약하다 to reserve, to make a booking Ⓣ 56, 131, 132, 134, 142, 166 Ⓢ 38, 96, 98, 107

예약한 사람 이름을 말하다 to give the name of the person who made the booking Ⓢ 107

예절 etiquette Ⓣ 77, 166 Ⓢ 54

오랜만에 in a long time Ⓣ 68, 86, 87, 149, 150, 156, 157, 169 Ⓢ 109, 113, 117

오랫동안 for a long time Ⓣ 24, 25 Ⓢ 49, 62, 63

오른쪽으로 가다 to go right Ⓢ 67, 79

오피스텔 officetel Ⓣ 167 Ⓢ 83

오히려 rather Ⓣ 125

옥 jade Ⓣ 89

올림픽 Olympics Ⓣ 26 Ⓢ 16

올림픽대로 Olympic Highway Ⓣ 101, 167 Ⓢ 74, 79

옮기다 to move Ⓣ 110, 114~116, 118 Ⓢ 86, 93

옷차림 outfit Ⓣ 20, 25, 33, 42, 43, 77, 164 Ⓢ 22, 23, 29

완료되다 to be completed Ⓣ 168

왕복 round-trip Ⓣ 130 Ⓢ 107

외국인 등록증 certificate of alien registration Ⓣ 30, 31, 58, 67, 165

외국인등록증을 내다 to give one's alien registration card Ⓢ 51

외롭다 to be lonely Ⓣ 158, 159

외식하다 to eat out Ⓣ 38

왼쪽으로 가다 to go left Ⓢ 79

요금 fee Ⓣ 60, 61, 104, 105, 167, 168 Ⓢ 51, 78

욕실 bathroom Ⓢ 25

욕심이 많다 to be greedy Ⓣ 161

용기 courage Ⓣ 157 Ⓢ 117

용돈 allowance (pocket money) Ⓣ 38 Ⓢ 24

우등 deluxe Ⓣ 95 Ⓢ 79

우등 고속버스를 타다 to take a deluxe express bus Ⓢ 79

우선 first Ⓢ 59

우정 friendship Ⓣ 89

우편물 mail Ⓣ 158, 160

우표 stamp Ⓣ 58, 59 Ⓢ 51, 102

우표를 붙이다 to put a stamp on Ⓣ 59 Ⓢ 51

우회전하다 to turn right Ⓣ 96, 97 Ⓢ 71, 79

운전면허증을 내다 to give one's driver's license Ⓢ 51

울긋불긋 colorful Ⓣ 143

울다 to cry Ⓣ 29 Ⓢ 101

원룸 one-room (studio) Ⓣ 115

원망하다 to blame Ⓣ 35

원피스 dress Ⓣ 20, 25 Ⓢ 10, 23, 109

월드컵경기장 World Cup Stadium Ⓣ 93 Ⓢ 67

월세 monthly rent Ⓣ 113, 124, 135, 167 Ⓢ 84, 100

위치 location Ⓣ 58, 124

유산 inheritance Ⓣ 161

윷놀이 *yutnori* (traditional board game) Ⓣ 47, 165 Ⓢ 37

은색 silver Ⓢ 23

음성 메시지 voice message Ⓣ 149, 169 Ⓢ 111

음식을 차리다 to set the table Ⓣ 76, Ⓢ 37, 65

음악회 concert Ⓣ 75, 85, 140

음주 운전하다 to drink and drive Ⓣ 100 Ⓢ 79

의논하다 to consult Ⓣ 167

이대역 Ewha Womans University subway station Ⓣ 93, 96, 97 Ⓢ 67, 71

재학 증명서 **certificate of student enrollment** Ⓣ 58, 165 Ⓢ 51

재학증명서를 내다 **to give one's certificate of enrollment** Ⓢ 51

저고리 **Korean-style short coat** Ⓣ 168

저울 **(weighing) balance** Ⓣ 59, 60, 61 Ⓢ 42, 51

저울에 올리다 **to place on the scale** Ⓣ 59, 61 Ⓢ 42, 51

저울에 짐을 올리다 **to put on** 59, 60, 61

저자 **author** Ⓣ 65, 165 Ⓢ 51

저자를 검색하다 **to search the author's name** Ⓢ 51

전공하다 **to major in** Ⓣ 120, 121

전달하다 **to deliver** Ⓣ 74

전부 다 팔리다 **to sell out** Ⓢ 107

전세 ***Jeonse*** Ⓣ 113, 124, 167 Ⓢ 84

전자레인지 **microwave** Ⓣ 120, 121 Ⓢ 90

전체 **all** Ⓣ 65, 106, 165

전통 놀이를 하다 **to play traditional games** Ⓣ 46, 50, 51, 165 Ⓢ 37

전통의상 **traditional clothing** Ⓢ 16

전하다 **to deliver** Ⓣ 74, 78, 79, 154, 159 Ⓢ 56, 121

전해 주다 **to pass on** Ⓣ 78, 79, 156–158 Ⓢ 38, 117

절약하다 **to save (time, cost)** Ⓣ 95, 104, 167

절을 하다 **to bow** Ⓢ 32, 121

점퍼 **jacket** Ⓢ 18, 23

접다 **to fold** Ⓣ 31

정 **sentiment** Ⓣ 50, 51

정리하다 **to put in order** Ⓣ 56 Ⓢ 38

정문 **main entrance** Ⓣ 97, 149, 164 Ⓢ 71

정성껏 **sincerely** Ⓣ 161

정신없다 **to be distracted** Ⓣ 156–158 Ⓢ 117

정장 차림 **formal attire** Ⓣ 25 Ⓢ 29

정체되다 **to be congested (traffic, roads, etc)** Ⓣ 101, 103 Ⓢ 76, 79

정치학 **political science** Ⓣ 120, 121

정확하다 **to be exact** Ⓣ 22, 65, 87 Ⓢ 12

제기차기 **kicking the *Jegi*** Ⓣ 50, 51, 165 Ⓢ 35, 37

제목 **title** Ⓣ 65, 86, 104

제비 **swallow** Ⓣ 160, 161

제시간 **the appointed time** Ⓢ 73

조리 시설이 있다 **to have cooking facilities** Ⓢ 93

조리실 **kitchen** Ⓣ 119, 121 Ⓢ 93

조카 **nephew or niece** Ⓣ 41, 164 Ⓢ 12, 32

졸업식 **graduation** Ⓣ 23, 164

종류 **type** Ⓣ 83, 104

좌석 **seat** Ⓣ 131, 168 Ⓢ 107

좌회전하다 **to turn left** Ⓣ 96, 97 Ⓢ 71, 79

주머니 **pocket** Ⓣ 29, 31, 164

주문 **request, order** Ⓣ 96, 97, 137–139, 142, 168 Ⓢ 40, 72, 102, 104, 107

주문 예약을 받다 **to take advance orders** Ⓣ 138, 139 Ⓢ 107

주문하다 **to order** Ⓣ 137–139, 142, 168 Ⓢ 102, 104, 107

주변 **periphery** Ⓣ 96, 101, 106, 113, 122, 167 Ⓢ 93

주변 자연 환경이 좋다 **to have a good surrounding natural environment** Ⓢ 93

주변에 편의시설이 있다 **to have amenities nearby** Ⓢ 93

주변이 조용하다 **to have quiet surroundings** Ⓢ 93

주소를 적다 **to write down the address** Ⓢ 51

주의를 주다 **to give warning** Ⓣ 118

초록색(녹색) green Ⓣ 28, 50, 51, 106 Ⓢ 23

촛불을 끄다 to put out candles Ⓢ 37

촛불을 켜다 to light candles Ⓢ 37

최근 recent Ⓣ 137, 147

추수감사절 Thanksgiving Day Ⓢ 37

추억이 되다 to become a memory Ⓢ 121

축하 인사를 하다 to congratulate someone Ⓢ 121

출발지 place of departure Ⓣ 95, 97

출입국관리사무소 immigration service Ⓣ 165 Ⓢ 51

출퇴근하다 to attend work Ⓣ 117

출판사 publisher Ⓣ 53, 65, 71

취소되다 to be cancelled Ⓣ 79

취향 taste Ⓣ 81 Ⓢ 58

치다 to type Ⓣ 65 Ⓢ 46, 51

치와와 Chihuahua Ⓣ 164

친하다 to be close with Ⓣ 35, 68, 80, 86, 148, 153, 159 Ⓢ 57, 87

칠면조 고기를 먹다 to eat turkey Ⓢ 37

칠순잔치 70th birthday party Ⓢ 37

카드를 발급하다 to issue a card Ⓢ 51

카디건 cardigan Ⓢ 23

칸 space 65

캐주얼 casual Ⓣ 81 Ⓢ 58

커피 잔 coffee cup Ⓣ 84, 85, 88 Ⓢ 65

컴퓨터 마우스 computer mouse Ⓣ 164 Ⓢ 27, 37

케이크를 자르다 to cut the cake Ⓢ 37

코미디언 comedian Ⓣ 151

코트 coat Ⓣ 139 Ⓢ 23

코트를 입다 put on a coat Ⓢ 23

퀵 서비스로 배달하다 to deliver by motorcycle courier Ⓣ 139 Ⓢ 107

퀵서비스 fast delivery service Ⓣ 139 Ⓢ 107

크리스마스 Christmas Ⓣ 49 Ⓢ 37

크리스마스트리를 만들다 to decorate the Christmas tree Ⓢ 37

클릭하다 to click Ⓣ 65, 165 Ⓢ 46

키우다 to raise Ⓣ 57, 75 Ⓢ 39

탈의실 dressing room Ⓣ 168

택배 home delivery Ⓣ 96, 97, 138, 139 Ⓢ 71, 107

택배로 보내다 to send by courier Ⓣ 139 Ⓢ 107

택배비를 계좌로 보내다 to put the delivery fee into the bank account Ⓢ 107

택시를 잡다 to take a taxi Ⓣ 100 Ⓢ 79

토마토 tomato Ⓣ 136 Ⓢ 101

통로 자리에 앉다 to sit in an aisle seat Ⓢ 57, 107

통역 interpretation Ⓣ 112 Ⓢ 82

통장을 만들다 to open an account Ⓣ 62 Ⓢ 51

통학하기 편하다 to be convenient for commuting Ⓣ 117 Ⓢ 87, 93

통학하다 to attend school Ⓣ 117 Ⓢ 87, 93

투호 *tuho* (throwing arrows into a jar) Ⓢ 37

틀다 to turn on Ⓣ 167 Ⓢ 88

파란색 blue Ⓣ 28, 106 Ⓢ 13, 20, 23, 104

파랗다 to be blue Ⓣ 27, 164 Ⓢ 17

판단하다 to judge Ⓣ 32, 33

판매하다 to sell Ⓣ 139 Ⓢ 107

판사봉 judge's gavel Ⓢ 37

허리를 굽혀서 인사하다 to bow low Ⓢ 121

헤어지다 to break up Ⓣ 116, 150, 151 Ⓢ 86, 121

현금 인출기 automated-teller machine (ATM) Ⓣ 66, 67, 70, 134 Ⓢ 51, 99

현금 인출기에서 확인하다 to check at the ATM Ⓢ 51

현금 카드를 만들다 to make a cash card Ⓣ 66, 67 Ⓢ 47, 51

현금으로 계산하다 to pay in cash Ⓣ 62 Ⓢ 43, 107

호텔을 알아보다 to look for a hotel Ⓢ 79

혹시 by any chance, possibly Ⓣ 25, 30, 31, 87, 157, 158 Ⓢ 13, 15, 17, 18, 20, 102

홈페이지에 서명을 치다 to input a name on the homepage Ⓢ 51

홈페이지에서 자료를 다운받다 to download materials from the homepage Ⓢ 51

화면 screen Ⓣ 165 Ⓢ 46

화살 arrow Ⓢ 27 137

화살표 arrow Ⓢ 49

화장지 tissue Ⓢ 62

확인하다 to verify Ⓣ 57, 66, 67, 74, 81, 96, 132, 133, 140, 141 Ⓢ 39, 46, 51, 52, 98, 107

환갑(회갑) 60th birthday party Ⓣ 52, 75 Ⓢ 37, 53

환영 인사를 하다 to welcome someone Ⓢ 121

환전하다 to exchange (money) Ⓣ 63

환절기 change of seasons Ⓢ 113, 119

활 bow Ⓢ 27, 37

활발하다 to be active Ⓣ 32, 33, 146, 164 Ⓢ 21, 22, 108

황금 gold Ⓣ 89

회복되다 to recover Ⓣ 75 Ⓢ 53, 65

회사에 취직하다 to get a job in a company Ⓣ 81, 157, 158 Ⓢ 53, 65

회사에서 승진하다 to get promoted at work Ⓢ 65

회색 gray Ⓣ 25, 28 Ⓢ 23

후식 dessert Ⓣ 83, 166

훌륭하다 to be great Ⓣ 35

훨씬 much more Ⓣ 35, 102, 103 Ⓢ 21, 75

휴게실 break room Ⓣ 111, 121 Ⓢ 81, 93

휴대 전화를 끄다 to turn off one's cell phone Ⓢ 107

휴지 tissues Ⓣ 84, 85, 88, 111 Ⓢ 65, 80, 81

흡연실 smoking room Ⓢ 57

About the Authors

김현진 Hyun Jin Kim
이화여자대학교 언어교육원 특임교수 Professor of Special Appointment, ELC, Ewha Womans Universiy
이화여자대학교 독어독문학과 박사
Ph.D. in Germans Linguistics, Ewha Womans Universiy

윤여옥 Yeo Ok Yoon
이화여자대학교 언어교육원 강사 Instructor of ELC, Ewha Womans Universiy
이화여자대학교 한국학과 석사 M.A. in Korean Studies, Ewha Womans Universiy

이은진 Eun Chin Yi
전 이화여자대학교 언어교육원 강사 Former Instructor of ELC, Ewha Womans Universiy
연세대학교 교육대학원 외국어로서의 한국어교육 전공 석사
M.A. in Korean Language Education as a Foreign Language, Yonsei University